JOHNNY CASH
THE SONGS

JOHNNY CASH

The Songs

Edited by Don Cusic

MAINSTREAM
PUBLISHING
EDINBURGH AND LONDON

Johnny Cash: The Songs
Introduction © Don Cusic

First published in the United States of America in 2004
by Thunder's Mouth Press

First published in Great Britain in 2005 by
MAINSTREAM PUBLISHING COMPANY (EDINBURGH) LTD
7 Albany Street
Edinburgh EH1 3UG

ISBN 1 84018 993 2 ⊢

A catalogue record for this book is available from
the British Library

Typeset in Apollo and Bookseller
Printed and bound in Great Britain by
Antony Rowe Ltd, Chippenham, Wiltshire

CONTENTS

INTRODUCTION 7

GOD 57

COWBOYS, INDIANS AND OUTLAWS 111

RAILROADS AND TRAINS 139

PRISONS AND PRISONERS 157

SOLDIERS AND WARS 173

PATRIOT 183

PEOPLE 195

MUSIC 229

PLACES 243

GROWING UP COUNTRY 265

TRAVELLIN' 279

LOVE GONE RIGHT 289

LOVE GONE WRONG 319

THE MAN IN BLACK 349

ACKNOWLEDGEMENTS 369

INDEX OF SONG TITLES 371

PERMISSIONS 375

INTRODUCTION

MAN IN BLACK AND WHITE:
The Songs of Johnny Cash

Johnny Cash was certainly a poet, but he was much more than that: he was a *writer*. He wrote a novel, *Man in White*, two memoirs, *Man in Black* and *Cash: The Autobiography*, a lot of liner notes on albums for himself and others, and dialogue for his albums, TV shows and movies. So this book of Johnny Cash's lyrics and the idea of looking at him as a poet is really only a partial glimpse of him as a writer. But it is an important part – probably the most important part – of Johnny Cash because, more than anything else, Johnny Cash was a singer of songs. These songs are like his children that he sent forth into the world, carrying a message he wanted to say or perhaps no message at all, just a story from which the listener took his or her own message. Sometimes they were just songs sung to tap your toes to and forget your troubles. Unlike many other songwriters, whose 'writing' consists of singing a song over and over and then putting it down on a tape recorder, Cash actually worked out the lyrics of his songs with pen and paper.

Looking at these songs as poetry is impressive; Cash always made sure his songs were well written, polished and complete. There are glimpses of Cash here, stories and episodes and feelings from his personal life, but he also had a strong, vivid imagination. In a lot of these songs Johnny Cash was a vessel for somebody else's story or feelings or message.

The story of Johnny Cash is rooted in the north-east corner of

Arkansas where he grew up. Ray and Carrie Cash were sharecroppers in Kingsland, Arkansas, during the Great Depression when their fourth child, J.R. Cash, was born on 26 February 1932. Three years later, the Cashes took their five children (a daughter, Reba, was also born in Kingsland) and moved to the Dyess Colony in north-eastern Arkansas, located on the Tyronza River. The Cash family arrived at their new farm on 24 March 1935.

The Dyess Colony was named after W.R. Dyess, the New Deal ERA administrator of Arkansas. This colony was created by President Franklin Roosevelt's New Deal in an attempt to help farmers during the Depression. Applicants were screened and 500 families were initially invited to a new home and twenty acres. If the family stayed and did well, they could purchase the land after three years; the Cashes did well and eventually owned forty acres. The land had thick black topsoil, a result of the Mississippi river flooding for years, so it was good cotton-growing land and the Cashes grew cotton there for almost twenty years. This is where Johnny Cash lived for fifteen years, from 1935 until 1950.

Johnny Cash joked that he 'grew up under socialism', a term that is often levelled at government-instigated programmes such as the New Deal in general and the Dyess Colony in particular. But people who are poor and desperate don't care about such terms; they only want to provide for their families and this colony gave Ray Cash an opportunity to provide for his family. He did well as a farmer, in spite of bouts of bad weather and bad luck. For J.R. (as Cash was called by his family, although the nickname 'Shoo-Do' was also used), the five-room white house became a loving, nurturing home and those fields provided a heritage of hard work.

To encourage her son, Carrie Cash bought a guitar from Sears Roebuck and tried to teach young J.R. to play, but he wasn't really interested and later sold it to another local boy. Instead, J.R. sat at the kitchen table every evening and listened to the radio.

That radio wasn't just music for idle time; it gave him inspiration and relief from the daily grind of farming, a dream and vision he would pursue. Johnny Cash heard these songs and wanted to be part of that world, part of those who help to lift others with music, who give the unheard person a voice; he wanted to be one of those who at least gave people a reason to believe that there is hope in this world, dreams to follow, or maybe just come comfort in the deepest parts of the soul.

At Johnny Cash's high school graduation in 1950 he stood and sang 'Drink To Me Only With Thine Eyes'. In the following weeks he tried some odd jobs around Arkansas, moved to Pontiac, Michigan, where he got a job in the automobile industry for two weeks at the Fischer Body factory, then returned home and worked in an oleomargarine factory where his father worked. Spurred by frustration at his own job prospects as well as the gathering war clouds in Korea, he went to Blytheville, Arkansas, and enlisted in the Air Force on 7 July.

Cash received his basic training at Lackland Air Force Base in San Antonio, Texas. After basic, he received training as a radio operator at Keesler Air Force Base in Mississippi and was sent to Landsberg, Germany, where he monitored air traffic.

During his tour in Germany, Cash also travelled to Italy and France before he returned home to Dyess on 4 July 1954 at the completion of his four-year stint. While in basic training in San Antonio, he had begun dating a high school senior named Vivian Liberto, and had corresponded with her often while in Germany. They were married on 7 August 1954, and moved to Memphis to set up house.

During the first twenty-two years of Johnny Cash's life, he was shaped by several factors. First, his rural upbringing in Arkansas on a cotton farm had given him the kind of background that served as a common thread for country boys in the Depression. The radio brought him country music, allowing him to hear songs and singers he wouldn't have been able to hear before and shaping his musical tastes. His family was very religious and the early exposure to church gave him a deep, abiding faith that was always a part of him. Lastly, the personal tragedy of his brother's death left a huge emotional gap in his life.

Jack Cash, two years older than John, was fourteen when he was

INTRODUCTION

pulled into the table saw while cutting fence posts at a sawmill. He lived for eight days before dying at home. Cash said that the memory of his brother was always with him during his entire life.

After Jack's death, John began writing stories and poems. An indifferent student with a strong, basic intelligence, Cash remembers that 'In school I spent a lot of time daydreaming, and soon began putting those daydreams down on paper.' He also began writing songs and, lured by magazine ads that promised to make stars of songwriting hopefuls, sent some of his songs away. 'I'd see the ads in the country song magazines and I'd send my poem off to them, and then they'd start sending me the feeders,' he told Christopher Wren. But 'they didn't get any of my money, because I couldn't raise it. That's the only reason I didn't send them money, though, because I didn't have it.'

Cash was also impressed by his big brother, Roy, who formed a country group in the late 1930s. Called the Delta Rhythm Ramblers, they performed locally and on KCLN in Blytheville.

In the Air Force, Cash had begun to play and sing country songs together with some friends in the barracks who called themselves the 'Landsberg Barbarians'. From this group, Cash was inspired to learn to play the guitar, so he bought a cheap German guitar for about five dollars and carried it back four miles to the barracks through a snowstorm. A friend taught him chords on the guitar and Cash soon began to play the songs of Hank Williams, Jimmie Rodgers, Ernest Tubb, Hank Snow, the Carter Family, Ray Acuff, and other country stars. Christopher Wren observes in his biography about Cash that 'His barracks buddies had catalysed his passion for country music. Now he was not just singing but also picking guitar into a German tape-recorder that he had bought at the base exchange. He was writing songs, too, and some of his lyrics were printed in the base newspaper.' (The song 'Hey, Porter' was printed as a poem in *Stars and Stripes*.)

Back in the States in civilian life, living in Memphis with his new wife, Johnny obtained a job with the Home Equipment Service on Summer Avenue as an appliance salesman and enrolled in the

Keegan School of Broadcasting on the GI Bill to learn how to be a radio announcer. Cash was never a very good salesman but the owner, George Bates, liked him and asked what he really wanted to do. Cash replied he wanted to be a singer and Bates asked what it would take to sing on the radio. Cash replied he needed a sponsor who would pay fifteen dollars for a fifteen-minute radio show; Bates agreed to sponsor Cash on a Saturday afternoon show 2.00 to 2.15 over KWEM in Memphis. The show lasted two months and Cash received a few bookings around Memphis from the show.

By this time Cash had joined Luther Perkins and Marshall Grant, two mechanics who worked at Hoehn Chevrolet Automobile Sales garage where Cash's brother, Roy, worked as night-service manager; Roy had told his brother about the two musicians. Grant, who was the day-service manager, Perkins (described as 'a genius on generators, starters and voltage regulators') and Cash soon got together and began practising. Marshall Grant remembers that 'The first night we got together, it was at Luther's on Nathan Street. Johnny played and sang Hank Snow's "Moving On", and we played along, too.' Grant added that 'We looked forward to getting together. Our wives would play canasta and talk and drink coffee.' One night Cash suggested Perkins and Grant each play different instruments; Perkins began to play lead guitar and Grant picked up the bass (originally they all played acoustic guitars). Thus, Cash's original back-up group, the Tennessee Two, was born.

Johnny Cash had a burning ambition to hear himself singing on the radio and was aware of Sun Records in Memphis, a small recording studio and label located on Union Avenue, and its owner and founder, Sam Phillips. One day Cash called Scotty Moore, Elvis's guitar player, and asked how to get an audition with Phillips; Moore told him to just go to the studio, so Cash began to stop by Sun Records in hopes of meeting Phillips. After a number of times when Phillips wasn't in or was in a meeting or otherwise occupied, Cash finally saw him, introduced himself and asked for an audition; Phillips invited him in and Cash sang a number of songs for him. Probably during this meeting, in late 1954, Phillips recorded two songs with just Cash and his guitar, 'Wide Open Road' and 'You're

My Baby' (sometimes known as 'Little Woolly Booger'). Later, Cash came back with Luther Perkins and Marshall Grant and they auditioned. At this point the group viewed itself as a gospel group and Cash wanted to do gospel material, but Phillips was reluctant to record gospel because Sun couldn't sell it; the future for the record company was in what became known as rockabilly. Cash quickly realised this and during this audition, probably in early 1955, Sam Phillips recorded them doing 'Folsom Prison Blues', 'Hey, Porter', 'Wide Open Road', 'Two-Timin' Woman', 'Port of Lonely Hearts' and 'My Treasure', all of which Cash had written, and 'Goodnight Irene', which had been a big hit in 1950 for the Weavers. In February, Cash, Grant and Perkins went back into the studio and recorded 'Wide Open Road', 'Cry, Cry, Cry' (which he had written since the last session), and 'Hey Porter'; the last two would be his first single release from Sun, with 'Cry, Cry, Cry' entering the *Billboard* country chart on 26 November and reaching number fourteen.

Although the record did not enter the national chart until November, it had been released in June and Cash spent the summer performing wherever he could in and around Memphis. It was a regional hit at first, selling about 100,000 copies in the south-east, and opened the door for Cash to play shows. He played in movie theatres during intermissions, in school auditoriums, and in the Overton Park shell in Memphis on a show with Elvis Presley. A small taste of 'road fever' was all it took for Cash to want to perform live all over the country, but he first needed to pick up any dates he could. Cash remembers: 'I got in my Plymouth and drove all over north-eastern Arkansas, dropping in at theatres and schoolhouses, asking them if I could book myself in there to play a show.'

On Cash's third Sun session he recorded 'Folsom Prison Blues', 'Luther Played the Boogie', 'So Doggone Lonesome' and 'Mean-Eyed Cat', all songs he'd written. His second single, 'So Doggone Lonesome', was released in December 1955 and entered the *Billboard* charts on 4 February 1956, followed a week later by 'Folsom Prison Blues'; both songs rose to the number-four position.

Just after the second single was released, Cash quit his job selling appliances and dedicated himself to making a living playing music. Since the dates were coming more often, and further away from Memphis, and since he wanted Luther Perkins and Marshall Grant with him, the musicians had to make a critical decision. Unlike Cash, they had good jobs making good salaries that provided security for themselves and their families, so they had a lot to lose. For Marshall Grant the problem was solved by not quitting his job but rather taking a leave of absence for six months; Perkins did the same. They were such good mechanics that the auto shop would give them back their jobs if things in the music business didn't pan out.

The third single for Johnny Cash on Sun Records would be the one that would catapult him to stardom: 'I Walk the Line' was recorded on 2 April 1956 and released in May. It entered the *Billboard* charts the following month, moved to number one and stayed on the charts for forty-three weeks, selling well over a million singles.

The song hit during the same period in which Elvis was achieving superstardom; Presley would sell over ten million records this year, be seen on national television, and appear in his first movie. His music would become the source of sermons by preachers and admonitions by teachers and parents.

The success of Elvis was, in part, responsible for the success of Johnny Cash. Elvis was the first Sun artist to hit big and his success created interest in the small label. When Sam Phillips sold Elvis's contract to RCA in the autumn of 1955 for $40,000, part of that money went into promoting Johnny Cash, whose second single was released at the end of that year. Musically, Cash was influenced by Elvis's guitar playing, using the full, strong rhythm himself. But Elvis would move over into pop and then 'rock 'n' roll', the category of charts created after the success of artists like the Sun group, while Cash would remain in country music, although some of his records crossed over into the pop charts.

The reason was fairly simple: Elvis's talent lent itself to rock 'n' roll; Cash's did not. Cash has a strong, unique voice but it is rooted in country and he could never be a screamer or shouter. The sound of Cash and the Tennessee Two was unique and different, but they were limited. As Marshall Grant observed, 'We didn't work to get that boom-chicka-boom sound. That's all we could play.'

After 'I Walk the Line', Cash had a series of hit records for Sun: 'There You Go', 'Ballad of a Teenage Queen' and 'Guess Things Happen That Way' all went to number one, while 'Train of Love', 'Next in Line', 'Home of the Blues', 'Big River', 'Come in Stranger', 'The Ways of a Woman in Love' and 'You're the Nearest Thing to Heaven' were all top ten. ('Give My Love to Rose', also during this period, reached number thirteen.) In July 1958, Cash had his last recording session for Sun and began recording for the major label Columbia Records. Cash and Carl Perkins had been approached by Don Law, head of Columbia's country recording in Los Angeles in the summer of 1957; Cash signed his Columbia contract on 1 November of that year but, because of his Sun contract, it would not take effect until 1 August 1958. Cash's first Columbia session was in Nashville on 24 July 1958, and his first release was a two-sided hit: 'All Over Again' reached number four, while 'What Do I Care' reached number seven. His next single, 'Don't Take Your Guns to Town', reached number one and, although his old label, Sun, continued to release records through 1960, Cash's career increasingly reflected the songs released by Columbia: 'I Got Stripes', 'Ring of Fire', 'The Matador', 'Understand Your Man', 'Ballad of Ira Hayes', 'Bad News' and 'The One On the Right is On the Left'.

Much has been written about Johnny Cash's drug addiction during the 1957–67 period. He briefly began taking amphetamines in 1957 as a way of coping with the demands of the road, having to stay up for the long nights of travelling and then perform; tranquillisers became necessary in order to get some rest. In 1967 Cash isolated himself in his home on Old Hickory Lake and, with the help of Mother Maybelle Carter, June Carter and Dr Nate Winston, went through the withdrawal process to overcome his addiction. On 11 November 1967, he gave his first concert without the help of pills (a fund-raising event at Hendersonville High School, near where he lived), and on 1 March 1968 he married June Carter. The following year they had a son, John Carter Cash, and Johnny Cash's career

JOHNNY CASH THE SONGS

shifted into overdrive with a string of million-selling albums, beginning with his *Folsom Prison* release, his network TV show on ABC and then his move, *Gospel Road*, filmed in Israel. To some it seemed that overnight Johnny Cash and arrived, but that is misleading.

During the ten-year period that was Cash's personal night of the soul, he also put together one of the best travelling groups in country music; his band had grown to include drummer W.S. Holland, then Carl Perkins, the Carter Family, and the Statler Brothers. He also recorded a number of important albums and had successful singles during this period, so on one hand it was an incredibly productive time for him. Despite his bouts with drugs, he also managed to write some important and memorable songs.

There were two musical revolutions in the 1950s: the rock revolution and the folk revolution. The starting point for the rock revolution can be placed in mid-1955, when Bill Haley and the Comets hit the top of the charts with 'Rock Around the Clock'. The starting point for the folk revolution can be placed in mid-1958, when the Kingston Trio hit the top of the charts with 'Tom Dooley'. Obviously, these musics existed long before these songs and these dates; however, these particular recordings pulled each music into a sharp focus and indicated the beginning of a mass awareness as well as a mass commercialism.

The two musical revolutions pulled on country music from two different directions; ultimately both would help country, but at first rock pulled artists and sales away from country, while folk music eventually brought some sales and credibility to country. Interestingly, as many of Cash's contemporaries moved towards rock, Cash moved towards the folk roots of country. He had an interest in folk music, performed and recorded a number of folk ballads, and audiences increasingly saw him as a folk performer. And since folk music was viewed as more 'intellectual', Cash got respect and attention from the college audience, which was normally not receptive to country.

The folk movement was interested in issues; the civil rights struggle and Vietnam were the two most obvious subjects for folk-music performers in the early 1960s. Cash became known for his focus on Indians and prisoners initially during this period, giving credibility to his music and setting him apart from other singers just pursuing a hit record. Ironically, Cash was able to do both: he had hit records as well as voiced his concerns, articulated issues, and made statements in songs.

THE SONGS OF JOHNNY CASH

The earliest examples of Johnny Cash's songs on recordings are on the Sun tapes. The first two songs he recorded (with just himself and his guitar) are 'Wide Open Road' and 'You're My Baby' (aka 'Little Woolly Booger'). Both represent an artist trying to find his voice; neither is a particularly memorable song, although Cash has characterised 'You're My Baby' as 'the worst thing I ever conceived'. It represents Cash trying to fit into the Sun rockabilly group rather than finding his own distinctive voice. 'Wide Open Road' is interesting because it shows Cash developing an idea so well. A common problem for beginning songwriters is not finishing an idea, getting through two verses and a chorus with some weak lines and calling it quits. But Cash has four strong verses and even changes the lyrics in his chorus the second time he sings it.

Other songs from early Sun tapes in late 1954 or early 1955 are 'Folsom Prison Blues', derived from the song 'Crescent City Blues' by Gordon Jenkins (which gives an early indication of Cash's later interest in prisoners); 'Two-Timin' Woman', a song about a man flexing his muscles to put a woman in her place; and 'Port of Lonely Hearts', which uses the metaphor of a ship and a storm to talk about love. It is interesting (though a bit odd) that Cash, who grew up with no ocean in sight, would use this metaphor, but it is effective. In 'My Treasure', Cash presents the moral lesson of a man who has lost perspective of the real treasures of life. Like the later 'I Walk the

Line', he pledges fidelity to his true love and lets the listener know the depth of his religious beliefs that guide his life. These songs are the earliest recordings with the Tennessee Two, Marshall Grant and Luther Perkins, and indicate a group working together to form a 'sound', experimenting in the studio. Many also show a deep, serious concern for moral issues – and a commitment to see issues in a moral right – that permeates the songs written by Johnny Cash.

Part of the sound that emerged came from limitations, particularly Luther Perkins' abilities as a lead guitarist. Perkins tried to play both lead and rhythm, plunking out a melody or lead line on the bass strings of his guitar and then muffling them with the heel of his hand to deaden them for the boom-chicka-boom sound. Another part came from improvisation. Since the group did not have a drummer or any percussion, Cash put a piece of paper on the neck of his guitar between the strings and the frets that created a 'rattle' when he strummed rhythm.

During the period Cash was on Sun (1955–58), he recorded twenty-eight songs he wrote. Of these songs recorded originally for Sun, a number stand out. 'Cry, Cry, Cry' was written specifically for a session; the idea came from a line used by disc jockey Smilin' Eddie Hill who used to say on his Memphis radio programme, 'We're going to squall and bawl and climb the walls'. A portion of that phrase, 'Squall and Climb the Walls', was the song's original title.

'I Walk the Line' was Cash's breakthrough song, becoming a national hit on both the country and pop charts and establishing him as a superstar within two years of his first Sun recordings. He recorded it on 2 April 1956. Cash told how he came to write the song to Christopher Wren for the biography *Winner's Got Scars, Too*:

> I had a tape recorder when I was in the Air Force in Germany. I went on duty one night and came back, and found somebody had been playing around with it. I turned it on and I heard, like someone was playing an organ, and at the end, somebody said: 'father'. I had all the boys in the barracks listen to it, and nobody knew what it was. I called a couple of Catholic boys in, because I thought it might be

like a mass. We couldn't figure it out. I'd dream about it at night, and with that weird melody, I kept it around six months.

Then one day I was fooling around on the tape recorder and I put it on backwards. I heard a guitar. And they'd been fooling around with my tape recorder, practising guitar runs. One of them said, 'Turn it off', and that played backwards was 'father' as clear as you could hear. And I called the whole barracks in and everybody had a big laugh.

Well, I just started practising those guitar runs. At the end of each run, I'd start saying, 'Because you're mine, I walk the line'. The melody sounded so haunting I thought it could be a hymn or love song.

I forgot about it till I was in a little town in East Texas, in a dressing room with Carl Perkins. I wrote the words down that night. The guitar run was that tape played backwards. I never had a more weird experience.

In his autobiography, Man in Black, Cash talks about writing the song and where the idea originated: 'I want to write a song that has something to say. A song that will have a lot of meaning not only for me, but for everybody who hears it – that says I'm going to be true not only to those who believe in me and depend on me, but to myself and to God – a song that might give courage to others as well as myself.'

Cash adds: 'The song came easily. It was one of those rare times I've felt a song was just "begging to be written" . . . The lyrics came as fast as I could write, and in twenty minutes I had it finished.' He said that Carl Perkins suggested the title 'I Walk the Line' after Cash had discussed several titles, including that one.

The lyrics are interesting because Cash uses an aaa rhyme scheme for the verses, with the fourth line containing an internal rhyme ('Because you're mine, I walk the line') to conclude each verse. This is the song that launched Cash to superstardom; it sold several million copies and was a hit in the country and pop fields. With this song, Johnny Cash firmly established himself as a recording artist and songwriter.

Other interesting early songs include: 'Give My Love to Rose', a story song and the first song he wrote and recorded with a western theme; 'Get Rhythm', a rockabilly number inspired, no doubt, by the rock 'n' roll phenomena; 'Straight A's in Love', where Cash uses the metaphor of a school report card to write a love song; 'Train of Love', the first song where Cash used the imagery of a train with lost love; 'Come In, Stranger', a song about his early life on the road; and 'Country Boy', a sentimental look at life in the country. In this last song, Cash seems already to be lamenting his lost life in the country: however, even though he envies the country boy who's fishing and free, he had clearly chosen to live in the city and chase his dreams of stardom far away from the idyllic country life. Country life is best viewed from a distance, and by this time Johnny Cash had put some distance between himself and the boy he once was.

Sun was primarily a singles company but it did put out two albums by Cash; in fact, the first Cash album, *Hot and Blue Guitar*, was the first album from Sun by *any* artist. The album sums up Cash's early work fairly well; it has 'Rock Island Line', 'I Heard That Lonesome Whistle', 'Country Boy', 'If the Good Lord's Willing', 'Cry, Cry, Cry', 'Remember Me', 'So Doggone Lonesome', 'I Was There When It Happened', 'I Walk the Line', 'Wreck of the Old '97', 'Folsom Prison Blues' and 'Doin' My Time'. Sun also put out a second album on Cash after he left, *Songs That Made Him Famous*, that included 'Ballad of a Teenage Queen', 'There You Go', 'I Walk the Line', 'Don't Make Me Go', 'Train of Love', 'Guess Things Happen That Way', 'The Ways of a Woman in Love', 'Next in Line', 'You're the Nearest Thing to Heaven', 'I Can't Help It', 'Home of the Blues' and 'Big River'.

Johnny Cash's first session for Columbia was on 24 July 1958, and his second was two weeks later, on 8 August. He had saved his newest compositions for these sessions, which explains why he recorded songs he didn't write on his last few Sun sessions (Jack Clement and Charlie Rich wrote a number of the songs Cash recorded). On his first Columbia session, Cash recorded five of his own compositions: 'Oh, What a Dream' (later renamed 'You Dreamer You'), 'I'll Remember You', 'Drink to Me', 'What Do I Care' and 'It

Was Jesus'. On his second session, he recorded 'Oh, What a Dream' and 'I'll Remember You' again, along with 'Run Softly, Blue River', 'All Over Again' and 'Frankie's Man, Johnny'. On his third session, 13 August, he recorded 'Lead Me Father', 'I Still Miss Someone', 'One More Ride', 'Pickin' Time' and 'Don't Take Your Guns to Town'.

The last two songs are interesting because on 'Pickin' Time' Cash wrote about his childhood and his life back on the farm. On 'Don't Take Your Guns to Town', Cash wrote about a western movie. The whole country was crazy about westerns and Johnny Cash was certainly part of this. Additionally, he had grown up watching 'B' westerns and singing cowboys in Arkansas; one of his heroes was Gene Autry. 'Don't Take Your Guns to Town' tells the story of a young man between grass and hay who strapped on some guns and headed to town; his mother warned him not to take his guns to town but the young man thought he was big enough to handle any situation. Well, the inevitable happened: he got into an argument with an experienced gunslinger and was shot down.

Of the rest of the self-penned songs he recorded, the most interesting one is 'I Still Miss Someone', which was originally a poem written by Johnny's brother, Roy, which Johnny put to a melody. 'Frankie's Man, Johnny' is a rewrite of the old folk ballad 'Frankie and Johnny', with the mention of a 'long-legged guitar picker', while 'Run Softly, Blue River' is a rewrite of the Robert Burns classic, 'Flow Gently, Sweet Afton'.

One of the reasons Cash signed with Columbia was that they promised he could do a gospel album; his second album for the label, *Hymns By Johnny Cash*, fulfilled that promise. On that album, recorded mostly on 13 January 1959, Cash recorded 'Are All the Children In', 'I Call Him' (co-written with his brother, Roy Cash) and 'He'll Be a Friend'.

'He'll Be a Friend' uses two biblical stories – of Noah and the Ark and Samson – to illustrate God's connection to man. 'I Call Him' is about God's faithfulness, while 'Are All the Children In', written to the melody of 'Just As I Am', uses the metaphor of mankind as God's children, illustrated by a mother's love for her children.

On 12 March 1959 Cash recorded 'I Got Stripes', 'You Dreamer

You', 'Five Feet High and Rising', 'The Man on the Hill', 'Hank and Joe and Me', 'The Caretaker', 'Old Apache Squaw', 'Don't Step on Mother's Roses', and his own arrangements of 'I Want to Go Home', 'The Great Speckled Bird' and 'My Grandfather's Clock'. This session perhaps sums up Johnny Cash and gives a preview of his entire career. 'Five Feet High and Rising' is a story from his childhood based on the Mississippi flood of 1937 that occurred about a month before Cash's fifth birthday. During this flood, the Cashes had to abandon their home and Cash's mother took the youngest children out first. They travelled by train from Kingsland to Stuttgart, Arkansas. Cash remembers that his mother 'had dressed me in my new suit. I kept running up and down the aisles. Down near Stuttgart, Arkansas, we weren't moving over five miles an hour, because the water was clear over the tracks. They were afraid they might hit a big log across the tracks if they went faster. I remember a lot of the women and children were crying because they were so worried and upset.'

'Hank and Joe and Me' is a western song about men searching for gold in the desert; 'Old Apache Squaw' shows his early interest in Indians; 'I Got Stripes' shows his interest in prisons and prisoners; 'My Grandfather's Clock' and the gospel number 'The Great Speckled Bird' are both old songs considered 'folk'. These songs came out on an album, *Songs of Our Soil*, which was his first 'concept' album.

From the beginning, Johnny Cash often used the melodies of old folk songs, often rewriting the lyrics or taking the basic idea and creating a new song. This is part of the folk tradition of songwriting, where creativity is synthesis. Nobody really starts with a blank sheet of paper or a blank slate; every song written is influenced by songs the songwriter has heard before. Synthesis is the very basis of creativity and the use of old songs to create new ones is a perfect example of this. Johnny Cash has been especially good at knowing old folk songs and using them in new ways, often with new lyrics he has written, to create new songs.

Cash's next album for Columbia, *Now There Was a Song*, does not contain any originals, but on his following album, *Ride This Train*,

JOHNNY CASH THE SONGS

recorded early in 1960, Cash developed the idea of a 'concept' album further. On this album he composed 'Dorraine of Ponchartrain', 'Going to Memphis' (a rewrite of an old folk song) and 'When Papa Played the Dobro'. There were no hit singles from this album but it was a landmark album for Cash. The folk movement was a lyric-dominated music interested in issues and topics deeper than a hit song. Cash's concept album lent itself to this folk movement. 'Dorraine of Ponchartrain' is the tragic story of a lover who drowns after a quarrel, slightly reminiscent of folk songs such as 'Barbara Allen'. 'Going to Memphis' is a folk-blues song about a man escaping from prison, while 'Papa Played the Dobro' is somewhat autobiographical, with the allusion to his father being a 'hobo' who struggled to support his family.

After *Ride This Train*, Cash recorded another gospel album, *Hymns From the Heart*. On this album there are no originals.

In late 1960 Cash recorded three other songs he had written, 'Five Minutes to Live', 'Locomotive Man' and 'Smilin' Bill McCall'. 'Five Minutes to Live' was written for a movie by the same title that Cash had a role in. (The title was later changed to *Door to Door Maniac* and the song was deleted.) 'Smilin' Bill McCall', a title that sounds a lot like the Memphis disc jockey Cash used to listen to, Smilin' Eddie Hill, is about a disc jockey who's a big hero on the radio – a sex symbol to the fans – but in person is four feet tall and bald.

Early in 1961 Cash recorded two more songs he had written; 'Forty Shades of Green', a beautiful song inspired by a trip to Ireland, and 'The Big Battle'. The latter is a Civil War song but also about war in general and is reminiscent of Stephen Vincent Benet's poem 'War is Kind'. In this song the soldier must face the reality of war. After the deaths of those who fought on the battlefield, there will be battles fought at home to conquer the grief and loss of loved ones. It is a powerful anti-war song, written before the Vietnam war was really part of American life.

Back in California in 1961, Cash's family moved from Encino to Casitas Springs. At the end of the year he hired June Carter as part of his show. The two had originally met in 1955 backstage at The Grand Ole Opry. June was part of the Carter Family and a well-known comedienne; she was hired on 7 December 1961 and first performed with the show in Dallas, where her role was to sing some songs solo, do some comedy, sing harmony and add a female face to what was becoming almost a variety-type show starring Johnny Cash.

In 1962 Cash recorded five songs he wrote: 'You Remembered Me', 'Little at a Time', 'Shamrock Doesn't Grow in California', 'Hardin Wouldn't Run' and 'Send a Picture of Mother'. Two of his self-penned songs, 'You Remembered Me' and 'Sing It Pretty, Sue', were on the album *Sound of Johnny Cash* released that year. 'You Remembered Me' is a love song from an unfaithful husband to a loving wife; 'Sing It Pretty, Sue' is about a man who loves a singer – but walks away so he will not be a burden as she climbs to stardom.

In the summer of 1962 Cash recorded another concept album, *Blood, Sweat, Toil and Tears*. Cash did not write any of these songs except 'Legend of John Henry's Hammer', where he took the basic folk song of 'John Henry' and turned it into a dramatic eight-minute masterpiece that shifted tempos and brought this story vividly to life. This album also contained songs such as 'Casey Jones', 'Busted', 'Another Man Done Gone' and the Jimmie Rodgers classic, 'Waiting For a Train'.

In 1963 Johnny Cash began a string of top single hits for Columbia, beginning with 'Ring of Fire', written by June Carter and Merle Kilgore, and 'The Matador' (written by Cash and June Carter), both that year; 'Understand Your Man', 'The Ballad of Ira Hayes' and 'Bad News' in 1964; 'Orange Blossom Special', 'The Sons of Katie Elder' (the title track from the movie of the same name) and 'Happy To Be With You' in 1965; and 'The One On the Right is On the Left' in 1966. His album *Ring of Fire* was a huge success, and it contained songs such as the TV theme song 'The Rebel – Johnny Yuma' and the title track (neither of which he wrote), in addition to the self-penned 'I'd Still Be There' (written with Johnny Horton), 'What Do I Care', 'I Still Miss Someone', 'Forty Shades of Green', 'The Big Battle' and 'Tennessee Flattop Box'. There were also two gospel songs, 'Peace in the Valley' and 'Were You There', on this album. In terms of a collection of self-penned songs, this was his strongest album so far and Cash was a commercial as well as critical success; this album was Cash's first to go 'gold' (sales of half a million units).

At the end of 1963 Cash released a Christmas album, *The Christmas Spirit*, that contained the self-penned songs 'The Christmas Spirit', 'The Gifts They Gave', 'We Are the Shepherds' and 'Who Kept the Sheep?'. 'The Christmas Spirit' is a recitation in which Cash recounts a dream where he is in Germany, Israel and Paris, and finds the true meaning of Christmas in the warmth of people and the Bible story of the birth of Christ. 'The Gifts They Gave' is a rewrite of an old folk song; 'We Are the Shepherds' is about the birth of Jesus from the point of view of the shepherds; and 'Who Kept the Sheep?', written with Mother Maybelle Carter's husband, Ezra, also tells the story of Christ's birth from this same point of view.

In 1964 Johnny Cash had a number-one hit with his song 'Understand Your Man'. This song had been recorded at the end of 1963 and was inspired by Bob Dylan's song, 'Don't Think Twice, It's Alright'. This song was included on the 1964 album, *I Walk the Line*, which also included the songs 'Folsom Prison Blues', 'Give My Love to Rose', 'Hey, Porter', 'I Still Miss Someone' and 'Big River'. That album also went gold and continued Cash's reputation as a major commercial success in country music.

The widespread interest in cowboys may have spurred Cash's interest in Indians. He was part Cherokee, so there was a natural interest, but the 1950s and '60s also saw Indians and the Old West re-examined through a number of movies.

Johnny Cash had written 'Old Apache Squaw' in 1957 while in Tucson on tour and recorded it in 1959; it was released on the album *Songs of Our Soil*. But Cash's interest in Indians was spurred further when he heard Indian songwriter Peter LaFarge performing in 1963 in Greenwich Village at the Gaslight Club. This is the same evening Cash first met Bob Dylan.

Back in Nashville, Columbia promotion man and Cash's friend Gene Ferguson played him 'The Ballad of Ira Hayes', written by LaFarge. This song tells the story of an Arizona Pima Indian who was one of those who raised the flag at Iwo Jima, immortalised in a photograph and monument at Arlington National Cemetery. But when Hayes returned home he faced discrimination, humiliation and poverty. An alcoholic, Hayes died a tragic death, drowned in a ditch.

On 5 March 1964, Cash went into the studio and recorded 'The Ballad of Ira Hayes', a protest song in the era of protests. The song was released in July of that year and climbed to the number-three position on the *Billboard* charts, spending twenty weeks on the charts. On 29 and 30 June, Cash was back in the studio recording the rest of the album that would become *Bitter Tears*. During this same period of time, Peter LaFarge was in Nashville at the Race Relations Institute at Fisk University, where the subject of Indian injustice received attention. Johnny Cash landed in the midst of the civil rights movement by recording songs about Indians, although he also stood up for blacks and against the southern racism that was in the daily news during that time.

Cash's reason for recording a concept album about Indians – indeed, it was an angry album as much about civil rights and protest as about Indians per se – were artistic as well as commercial.

In addition to 'The Ballad of Ira Hayes', other songs on the album included 'Custer', 'Drums' and 'White Girl', all by Peter LaFarge, 'The Vanishing Race' by Johnny Horton, and four songs written by Cash: 'Big Foot', 'The Talking Leaves', 'Apache Tears' and 'Old Apache Squaw'. 'Big Foot' was written after Cash had visited Wounded Knee, South Dakota, site of the final Indian 'fight'. There, on 29 December 1890, the 7th Cavalry slaughtered a group of Indians who were led by Big Foot, a chief suffering from pneumonia at the time. Cash wrote this song in a car after leaving the Wounded Knee battlefield on his way to the Rapid City airport.

'The Talking Leaves' is the story of Sequoia, the Cherokee who developed a written language for his people; 'Apache Tears' is the story of the eradication of the Apache, who lived in the southern Arizona and New Mexico area and who were the last tribe subdued by the Army. 'Old Apache Squaw' is also the story of the Apaches told from the very human side of a woman who has seen her family, tribe and heritage killed.

In 1965 Cash released the album *Orange Blossom Special*, and the title cut became a hit, reaching number three on the country charts. The album had three Bob Dylan songs ('It Ain't Me, Babe', 'Don't Think Twice, It's Alright' and 'Mama, You've Been On My Mind') and one song that Cash wrote, 'You Wild Colorado'. In addition, Cash recorded the Irish folk song 'Danny Boy', the Carter Family's 'Wildwood Flower', Harlan Howard's 'The Wall', country hits 'The Long Black Veil' (Lefty Frizell had a hit with it in 1959), 'Springtime in Alaska' (Johnny Horton's version was also a hit in 1959), and two spirituals, 'Amen' and 'All God's Children Ain't Free'.

After the turmoil created by 'Ira Hayes' and the *Bitter Tears* album, 'You Wild Colorado' is a rather safe song. It is a paean to the Colorado River and shows his continuing interest in the West. It was recorded at the end of 1964 and, in many ways, gave a preview of the western album he would do the next year.

Johnny Cash's interest in the West and cowboys, which he originally expressed in songs like 'Give My Love to Rose' and 'Don't Take Your Guns to Town', led to a double album of cowboy songs, *Johnny Cash Sings the Ballads of The True West*, that he recorded in March 1965. This album includes a number of old cowboy classics, such as 'The Streets of Laredo', 'I Ride an Old Paint', 'Bury Me Not on the Lone Prairie' and 'Green Grow the Lilacs', as well as some original songs, 'Hiawatha's Vision', 'The Shifting, Whispering Sands', 'Hardin Wouldn't Run', 'Mean as Hell' and 'Reflections'.

In the liner notes to this album Cash states that the idea for the album came from his producer, Don Law, who also brought Cash some books about the West. Cash read the books, as well as back issues of the magazine *True West*, and talked about the West with people like Joe Austell Small, publisher of several western magazines. When Law called a few months later to ask about the western album, Cash began writing out ideas for songs, using some folk-song collections and the advice of Tex Ritter. Cash also spent time in the desert with his jeep, absorbing the landscape of the West, before he finished the album.

The album features narration by Cash between a number of songs and the songs he wrote show the diversity of the West. In

'Hiawatha's Vision', Cash used Longfellow's poem as a starting point to tell the story of the settling of the West by whites who displaced Indians. 'Hardin Wouldn't Run', written after Cash had read a biography of the famous outlaw, is a narrative of John Wesley Hardin's life and death. 'Mean As Hell' is a recitation about a pact with the Devil made in order to settle the West. The poem is long and involved and endlessly fascinating. Obviously, Cash knew the violence of the West and the dangers of the desert; this is not an area for the squeamish. In 'Reflections', the last song on the album, Cash again presents a recitation that captures the panoply of the West, the history of this vast, savage land and the tough, resilient people who lived there.

In addition to this western album, Cash sang the theme song to the movie *The Sons of Katie Elder*, which starred John Wayne. The song reached number ten in the charts in 1965.

After Columbia released the double album entitled *True West*, they edited the album down to a single album entitled *Mean As Hell* and released that, too. And so 1965 ended with Johnny Cash's image firmly established as a folk singer of the mythical West. The next year Johnny Cash would make a 180-degree turn and hit the charts with some wildly comedic songs.

'The One On the Right is On the Left' is a political song of sorts written by Jack Clement, Cash's old producer from the Sun days, who had moved to Nashville and would produce records for Cash off and on for the next thirty years. 'The One On the Right' pokes fun at political labels and provides some humour in the serious game of politics. This song was followed by 'Everybody Loves a Nut', also written my Clement, which has Cash proclaim that the world likes people a little off-centre and slightly weird. The album *Everybody Loves a Nut* contains the two previously mentioned songs as well as 'Dirty Old Egg Sucking Dog', 'Boa Constrictor' and 'The Bug That Tried to Crawl Around the World'. After all that seriousness of dealing with volatile issues, and in the midst of a swirl of controversy from issues he addressed and stands he took, Johnny Cash needed a good laugh.

The songs Cash wrote on this album were 'Austin Prison' and

'Please Don't Play Red River Valley'. Cash's forte is not humorous writing, and 'Please Don't Play Red River Valley' shows he had a sense of humour but that it was expressed more in an ability to have fun rather than side-splitting wit. In 'Austin Prison' Cash returns to the theme of a prisoner who should not be in jail; in the end he escapes with the jailer's friendly help.

Cash's following album was *Happiness Is You* and marked a return to his traditional country roots. He re-recorded his Sun hit 'Guess Things Happen That Way', did the Stonewall Jackson hit 'A Wound Time Can't Erase', and recorded a song made famous by Roy Acuff, 'Wabash Cannon Ball'. This album, recorded at the end of 1965 and early 1966, features four songs by Johnny Cash: 'Happiness Is You' and 'Cotton Pickin' Hands', both written with June Carter; 'Happy To Be With You', written with Merle Kilgore and June Carter; and 'The Frozen Logger', written with James Stevens. Of these four songs, 'Cotton Pickin' Hands' harkens back to his youth as it tells the story of a loving, hard-working couple whose life revolves around the cotton crop.

But this album seems to be a transitional album for Cash, whose next album was totally written by him. Titled *From Sea to Shining Sea*, it is a concept album that deals with life in America. It is an album of everyday life and history; it gives an indication of the move toward patriotic songs and albums that lay ahead for Johnny Cash. Recorded in March and April 1967, the album is an extension of the theme first introduced on *Ride This Train*.

A lot of people saw Johnny Cash as larger than life; he probably saw himself the same way. In his songs, albums and life he always projected a sense of vision, a sense of 'calling' and a higher purpose to his life and work. He had never been just another artist looking for the next hit or a singer just trying to get to the next gig. If Johnny Cash achieved the status of a great man it was because he had aspired to become a great man. He set high standards for himself – in his life and his work – and worked hard to fulfil them. Although he may have fallen short of greatness at times in his life and work, his vision was always there and he was able to continue his journey having learned his lessons. Few people carry the ambition and resolve to become a great man in their life; Johnny Cash was one of them.

In the liner notes to *From Sea to Shining Sea*, Cash explains some of his songs. He states that 'The Whirl and the Suck' was a place in the Tennessee River near Chattanooga where 'there were whirlpools and suckholes, and the water was swift and deep', something early settlers had to face in their small boats. There was another danger, too: the Nickajack Indians would often attack settlers from the banks of the river. Cash states he wrote his song 'a half-mile inside Nickajack Cave . . . This particular spot was a high, flat place around a bend from outside light.'

'The Walls of a Prison' was written to the tune of the old British ballad 'The Unfortunate Rake' after Cash and his troupe had performed at Folsom Prison. 'Shrimpin' Sailin'' was inspired by a trip he took on a shrimp boat near Tarpon Springs, Florida. 'The Flint arrowhead' and 'Another Song to Sing' were written in Gallatin, Tennessee, by a riverbank where Cash found a number of arrowheads. 'Another Song' is an interesting look at the obligations of fame, obligations that Cash both felt deeply and enjoyed. He states, 'there's always one more path that I must walk' and 'always another song to sing'. But, although he enjoyed the active life, he also longed for quiet solitude, and in the second half of the song he states, 'at other times I'd rather be alone/Where I could not be found when I was gone.' It was both a joy and a pain to be Johnny Cash, and occasionally he let those feelings show in a song.

Cash claimed that 'The Masterpiece' and 'Call Daddy From the Mine' had been written about ten years before this album was recorded – that would have been about 1960 – but then forgotten until he rediscovered the lyrics. 'The Frozen Four-Hundred-Pound Fair-to-Middlin' Cotton Picker' is the story of a man who wanted to pick 400 pounds of cotton and froze to death trying; it recalls Cash's own days in the cotton fields. 'You and Tennessee' was written about his future wife, June, and 'Cisco Clifton's Fillin' Station' was written about an actual filling station in Dyess, Arkansas, where Cash grew up. 'From Sea to Shining Sea', which opens and closes the album, was obviously written in order to tie

JOHNNY CASH THE SONGS

the concept together and shows the scope of Cash's vision of himself and his work.

Some of the songs for *Carryin' On With Cash and Carter* were recorded in May 1967, right after *From Sea to Shining Sea* – in fact, some of the songs on the *Carryin' On* album were recorded during some of the same sessions that songs for *From Sea to Shining Sea* were recorded – and give a full indication of Cash's growing love for June Carter and his involvement with her professionally and personally.

The album contains several songs written by Cash and June Carter – 'Oh, What a Good Thing We Had', 'Shantytown' and 'You'll Be Alright' – while Cash alone wrote 'No, No, No'. The hit single from the album was the duet, 'Jackson'. There are two songs made famous by Ray Charles – 'I Got a Woman' and 'What'd I Say'; a song written by Cash's long-time bass player, Marshall Grant – 'Long-Legged Guitar Picking Man'; a Bob Dylan song that had been recorded in 1964 – 'It Ain't Me, Babe'; and a song written by June, Helen and Anita Carter – 'Fast Boat to Sydney'.

'Oh, What a Good Thing We Had' is a song about looking back at a love 'gone bad'. 'Shantytown' is the story of a poor boy on the wrong side of the tracks loving the rich girl; 'No, No, No' tells essentially the same story. Perhaps the relationship of Johnny Cash and June Carter at this point in time may be seen here. Cash was on drugs and viewed himself as coming from 'the wrong side of the tracks', while June carried the rich heritage of the Carter Family with her. Still, he loved her and believed he could be part of that heritage. 'You'll Be All Right' tells the story of someone who lost their 'honeybee' and who must 'cry a little bit/And die just a little bit', and then be all right. It could have been a song about the end of Cash's first marriage which, by this point, was beyond hope and repair.

In 1966 Johnny Cash left his home in California for a tour and never really returned. Although he would go back occasionally for visits, he increasingly stayed in Nashville when not on the road, usually at either Mother Maybelle Carter's home or in an apartment he had rented and then in a house he bought on Old Hickory Lake.

Marital problems resulted in a divorce originally filed during this year and finalised in January 1968.

On 3 November 1967, Cash woke up in a jail cell in Georgia. During the following week he nearly drove his tractor into Old Hickory Lake. He was found by June Carter hugging a tree, covered with ice. Cash locked himself away in his home to rid himself of his pill addiction and on 11 November gave his first pill-free concert. On 1 March 1968, he married June Carter and a year later his son, John Carter, was born.

During this period the breakthrough album for the 'new' Johnny Cash was recorded. *Live at Folsom Prison* was recorded on 13 January 1968. But the roots of that album go deeper than that date. Cash performed his first concert before inmates in 1957 in Texas at the Huntsville State Prison; in 1958 he performed at San Quentin for the first time (with Merle Haggard in the audience); and in 1966 he first performed at Folsom Prison. Obviously, Cash had a song for this venue, 'Folsom Prison Blues', which he released as a single. The single hit number one, while the album sold between five and six million copies and marked the beginning of a period during which Cash would become an American institution.

In addition to the title track, other self-penned songs on this album were 'I Still Miss Someone', 'Send a Picture of Mother', 'Give My Love to Rose' and 'I Got Stripes'. Although this was not Cash's first performance in a prison, it was the first concert that was recorded and solidified his connection with prisons and prisoners and firmly established him as an artist who bucked the ordinary, aligned himself with the underdog, challenged the safe and sure path, and proved once again that here was a man who had something to say, a singer who stood for something.

Johnny Cash's strong religious faith played a major role in him overcoming his pill addiction and the 'new' Johnny Cash had a rebirth of his Christian faith. So, after the Folsom Prison concert, Cash and his crew went to Israel, where they recorded an album, *In the Holy Land*. This album contains a great deal of dialogue as Cash and his group travelled around the Holy Land, speaking into a tape recorder at various sites. Songs that Johnny Cash wrote for this album were 'Nazarene', 'Land of Israel', 'Come to the Wailing Wall', 'He Turned the Water Into Wine' and 'God is Not Dead'. The hit single from this album was 'Daddy Sang Bass', written by Carl Perkins, an old friend from the Sun days and a member of the Cash travelling show.

After his time in Israel, Cash returned to the United States and recorded another live album in a prison; this one at San Quentin on 24 February 1969. Self-penned songs on this album include 'I Walk the Line', 'Starkville City Jail', 'San Quentin' and 'Folsom Prison Blues'.

The song 'Starkville City Jail' was based on a real experience Cash had in 1966 after he had played Mississippi State University. He wrote it the day before the San Quentin concert just for the inmates. According to Cash, he left his motel room on foot to look for some cigarettes around 2 a.m.

> I was just walking down the sidewalk, looking for a cigarette machine in a gas station. I was grabbing flowers as I walked, picking a daisy here, a dandelion there. Somebody phoned the police. The police car came and pulled alongside. The police got out of the car and grabbed me by the arm and said, 'Get in!' I asked what for. 'Just shut up and sit down,' they said. They took me to the police station. I don't even know what they put me in for.
>
> They took me along a row of cells. I didn't see anybody else, but there were some others there. I saw them in the morning when they brought them out on the work gang. They left me there. I began kicking at the cell door. I broke my big left toe and sprained my ankle. I was so damned mad, I wasn't in pain. I guess I had a pill or two in me. It was one time I didn't deserve to be there.
>
> In the morning at eight, the chief sent somebody down to let me out. He was at the desk. He asked me what I was doing out at 2 a.m. picking flowers. I said I was only going for cigarettes. He said someone had said I was in the yard picking flowers, and they didn't know who I was, and were

sorry. They drove me back to the motel. I packed and left town.

The chief of police apologised to Cash but the singer still had to pay a fine of thirty-six dollars. At the San Quentin concert, Cash said to the inmates, 'Well, thirty-six dollars for picking flowers, and a night in jail. You can't hardly win, can you? No telling what you'll do if you pull an apple or sump'n.' And then he sang 'Starkville City Jail'.

This album showed Cash to be more belligerent than during the Folsom Prison concert, putting himself squarely on the side of the prisoners. The album expressed his own jail experience, his role as a spokesman for prisoners and other outcasts since the success of *Live at Folsom Prison*, and his own frustrations at being down and out, an outsider and outcast during his life. 'San Quentin', a song so popular that the audience demanded he perform it again as soon as he sang it, begins, 'San Quentin, you've been livin' hell to me', and concludes, 'San Quentin, I hate every inch of you.'

This album also had a number-one song, 'A Boy Named Sue', written by Shel Silverstein.

On 7 June 1969, *The Johnny Cash Show* became a weekly TV show on ABC-TV. The hour-long show was originally a summer series, broadcast on Saturday nights. In the fall of 1969 the show was moved to Wednesday evenings, where it continued its run until May 1971. The show was briefly revived as a summer series in 1976.

This popular television programme brought Johnny Cash into American homes each week and multiplied his fame. Again, he used this platform to do more than entertain: he had a 'Ride This Train' segment that combined history and geography, he featured gospel music, and he introduced performers such as Bob Dylan and Kris Kristofferson. With this TV show, Johnny Cash went from being a superstar in country music to an American icon and a figure in country music of almost mythic proportions.

During the 1967–70 period, Cash received a number of awards that brought him national attention: a 1967 Grammy (presented in February 1968) for his duet with June Carter on 'Jackson'; another

Grammy (1968) for his *Folsom Prison* album; and a host of awards in 1969 from the Country Music Association, including Entertainer of the Year, Male Vocalist, Album (*San Quentin*), Single ('A Boy Named Sue'), Vocal Group (with June), and the Founding President's Award for outstanding service to the CMA. The following year he won a Grammy for his liner notes on Bob Dylan's *Nashville Skyline* album.

In addition to his TV show, Cash made other notable appearances. In 1969 he toured Vietnam, singing for the troops, and in 1970 he performed at the White House for President Richard Nixon. But in 1971 he ended his TV show because of interference from network executives, who were too tempted by the show's success to trust Cash's taste or country music so they increasingly forced inappropriate guests and tried to cut out the core of the show. It was a busy time for Cash, who spent these two years in heavy public demand. This high-profile time yielded great rewards in terms of personal bookings and also fuelled his creative juices. Cash always thrived on activity and seemed to be at his most creative when he was busiest and shouldering major responsibilities. He recorded several important songs he wrote during this period, including 'Flesh and Blood', 'Man in Black' and 'What is Truth?'.

During the first summer of his TV show, Cash recorded several songs he wrote. 'Come Along and Ride This Train' was for the segment in the television show, and 'Route #1, Box 144' expressed Cash's sense of the Vietnam War's injustice. It is an anti-war song that deals with a young man with a family who is sent off to fight – and comes home in a box. 'See Ruby Fall' was written with Roy Orbison, 'Cause I Love You' was written about June Carter, and 'Southwind' is about a train that carries his lover away. These songs were released on the album *Hello, I'm Johnny Cash*. In addition to these songs, during this same time he made his first recording of 'You Are What I Need', which would later be re-recorded and re-titled as 'Flesh and Blood' and used in the movie *I Walk the Line*.

Cash's record label, Columbia, would also release a double album during this period, *The World of Johnny Cash*, which contained a number of pre-released material, including the self-penned 'I Still Miss Someone', 'Pickin' Time', 'Frankie's Man, Johnny', 'Legend of

John Henry's Hammer', 'When Papa Played the Dobro' and 'Sing It Pretty, Sue'.

In March 1970, Cash recorded 'What is Truth?', which connected him to the youth of the nation and once again made him a spokesman for the outcast – in this case, the long-haired youth of the day who represented a cultural gap and great division between the generations. But although this was a hit single, it would not be released on an album.

'What is Truth?' originally had twelve verses, but Cash edited the song to four when he recorded it. According to Cash, as related in his biography written by Christopher Wren:

> I was sitting around at TV rehearsal watching the First Edition and really digging it. Merle Travis said, 'They sure play funny music, don't they?' I decided to write a song with that.
>
> I'd read a book on Pontius Pilate, and wanted to write a song on what is truth. I got up at 6:30 and the wheels were still turning, so I made some coffee and sat and wrote the song. It just came real fast, as long as it takes me to write it down.
>
> I felt it, and I thought about that line, 'What is truth?', and I thought about the youth of today, and a lot of them – not all of them – are searching for truth.

Cash taped his TV show on the stage of the Ryman Auditorium and during tapings recorded a number of songs that were later released. In February 1970, he recorded songs for the album *The Johnny Cash Show*, which included the hit single 'Sunday Morning Comin' Down', written by Kris Kristofferson. Self-penned songs on this album include 'Come Along and Ride This Train' and 'I'm Gonna Try to Be That Way', which reflects Cash's religious commitment as well as awareness of himself as a role model. In this song, Cash compares himself to Jesus, saying Jesus 'knew how to live right/Tried to be a light/Gave everybody a helping hand', before saying, 'I'm gonna try to be that way.' Cash then states that Jesus 'never done anybody wrong/He tried to help everybody 'long' and 'He preached love and brotherhood/He went around doin' good.' Cash wanted himself to 'do the kind of things a man oughta do/Say the kind of things a man oughta say'.

In October 1970, Cash recorded the soundtrack for the movie *I Walk the Line*, which starred Gregory Peck and Tuesday Weld. On the soundtrack is 'Flesh and Blood' as well as the self-penned 'I Walk the Line', 'The World's Gonna Fall on You', 'Hungry', 'This Town', 'Cause I Love you', 'This Side of the Law' and 'Face of Despair'. In these songs Cash put himself as an underdog. 'Face of Despair' is especially interesting, with the picture it paints of an old farmer with a 'back that's bent from years of toil'.

The following day Cash and his band recorded the soundtrack for the movie *Little Faus and Big Halsey*, which starred Robert Redford and Michael J. Pollard. Although Carl Perkins wrote the title song, Cash wrote 'Rollin' Free' and 'Little Man'. Again, Cash related to the underdog; in 'Little Man' he notes, 'It seems like people would get tired of looking down on people/It seems like people got to have someone to kick around/Always feeling like they need to be looked up to/And always someone there when they look down.' It is a perceptive look at mankind. In 'Rollin' Free', he expresses the wish to not 'be tied to a load/That I can't carry over the road'. In the second verse he states, 'I'm not worried about who I am/Cause frankly I don't give a damn/Long as I can be where I want to be/And doin' what I want to do.' It is a declaration of independence that Cash makes in this song, which he concludes with 'get your hands off me/I'm rollin' free.'

On 10 December 1970, Cash and guitarist Norman Blake went into the studio and recorded some songs intended for the Apollo 14 space flight. These songs, 'These Are My People', 'Road to Kaintuck', 'Battle of New Orleans', 'Remember the Alamo', 'Lorena', 'Mean As Hell', 'Mister Garfield', 'The Big Battle', 'Come Take a Trip on My Airship' and 'This is My Land' were not used for the space trip but were later used for his *America* album.

The fame from the TV show seemed to increase Cash's self-confidence and awareness of himself. On 16 February 1971, he recorded 'Man in Black', which stated, in essence, that he was on the side of the downtrodden. In this song, he states he wears black for 'the poor and the beaten down/Livin' in the hopeless, hungry side of town', for 'the prisoner who has long paid for his crime' and 'for those who never read or listened to the words that Jesus said'. He concludes the song by saying, 'I'd love to wear a rainbow every day/And tell the world that everything's OK/But I'll try to carry off a little darkness on my back/Till things are brighter, I'm the man in black.'

Just as Cash's TV show was ending in late spring 1971, Columbia released the album *Man in Black* that contained the self-penned 'You've Got a New Light Shining in Your Eyes', 'Singin' in Viet Nam Talkin' Blues', 'Ned Kelly', 'The Preacher Said "Jesus Said"' and 'Dear Mrs'. Additionally, around the same time as this album's release, Cash also recorded the self-penned 'I'll Be Loving You', 'I Promise You' and 'Miss Tara', as well as the future single 'A Thing Called Love'. These latter songs Cash wrote would be released on the album *A Thing Called Love* after a greatest hits package, *The Johnny Cash Collection*, had been released.

Of these songs, 'Dear Mrs' is interesting because it tells the story of a prisoner who died from loneliness, having never received a letter from his loved one although he carried her picture with him constantly. It is a wrenching song about prison life. 'Ned Kelly' is about an Australian outlaw, while 'Singin' in Viet Nam Talkin' Blues' tells the story of Cash's tour of Vietnam and concludes that 'if I ever go back over there anymore/I hope there's none of our boys there for me to sing for' because they've all 'come back home to stay in peace'.

In June 1972, Cash recorded several more songs to complete the album *America*. The album has a good deal of narration and dialogue; it could almost be called a book when it was finished, as it told the story from Paul Revere's ride, through the move West, to the War of 1812, the story of the Alamo, the Civil War and on down to contemporary times. Songs written by Cash include 'Big Foot', 'The Big Battle', 'Come Take a Trip on My Airship', 'Reaching for the Stars' and 'These Are My People'.

The *America* album was followed by the *Johnny Cash Family*

Christmas album, which sounded like a warm evening filled with reminiscences from Cash's family and friends. It sounded like the Cash troupe gathered around the dinner table at Christmas with a guitar and shared some special moments. The album was actually recorded in July 1972 and featured one song Cash wrote, 'Christmas With You', which expresses his happiness in family life with June.

Johnny Cash Family Christmas was followed by the album *Any Old Wind that Blows*, which featured Cash's songs 'Kentucky Straight', Country Trash', 'The Ballad of Annie Palmer' and 'Welcome Back Jesus'. 'Country Trash' is slightly reminiscent of the Hank Williams song 'Everything's Okay', as well as Cash's own 'Pickin' Time', as he takes pride in his blessings. In 'Kentucky Straight' he tells how wonderful life is with his woman, because 'we rise up every mornin' with the chickens/And every minute we're livin'' back in their 'happy shack'.

'Ballad of Annie Palmer' is about a woman from Jamaica, where Cash had a vacation home. 'Welcome Back Jesus' is almost a prayer, with his confession, 'I'm trying to stay upon the right track', although 'the ways get hard/Temptations come and I sure get tired'.

Cash's next album consisted of a number of live recordings pieced together under the album title *Sunday Morning Coming Down*. There were no new songs on this album. The album seems to have been done in an effort to capitalise on the demand for albums from Johnny Cash and to buy some time until his next major project, which came out in 1973.

After his TV show ended in March 1971, Cash embarked on a project that had deep significance for him, the movie *Gospel Road*, which he financed himself. Cash felt called to do something in Israel to express his Christian rebirth and deep faith and had gone there in 1968 to record his album *In the Holy Land*. However, Cash did not feel the album truly fulfilled his dream, so he decided to do a whole movie, which he started filming in 1971. The first songs for this soundtrack album were recorded in October 1971 and included the self-penned 'He Turned the Water Into Wine' and the title song written by Christopher Wren.

There were more songs recorded in January 1972 and throughout

INTRODUCTION

the spring of that year until the album was finished and released, along with the movie, the next year. Songs written by Cash on the *Gospel Road* album are 'He Turned the Water into Wine', 'The Miracle Man' (with Larry Lee), 'Praise the Lord' and 'I See Men as Trees Walking'. This last song is written from the perspective of a blind man whose sight was restored by Jesus.

Gospel Road consumed a great deal of Cash's time and energy and strengthened his marriage and working relationship with June Carter. His following album, *Johnny Cash and His Woman*, featured duets on six of the ten songs. Songs Cash wrote on this album include 'Saturday Night in Hickman County' and 'Matthew 24 (Is Knocking at the Door)'. The first song is about life in a small Tennessee county where Cash owned a farm, and where folks are 'thankful just to be a-living/Thankful that tomorrow's Sunday/Sorry that the next day's Monday'. In 'Matthew 24', Cash talks about the end of the world, a prophecy concerning Russia ('the great bear from the northland') and the 'coming Prince of Peace'.

It's difficult to imagine Johnny Cash recording a 'children's' album, after all those intense albums about the West, Indians, America, and other heavy subjects, but he did. Actually the album, *Children's Album*, seems directed to his children, especially his son, John Carter, who was around five when the album was released. The album was obviously inspired by Cash's son; the first song recorded for this album, 'I Got a Boy and His Name is John', was recorded in May 1972. Cash had opened his own recording studio near his home in Hendersonville, Tennessee – 'House of Cash' – and this was the first self-penned song he recorded in the studio. Other Cash songs on the album are 'Miss Tara', written for his daughter, 'Little Magic Glasses', 'Dinosaur Song', 'Tiger Whitehead' (written with Nat Winston), 'Little Green Fountain' – which lists young John Carter Cash as a co-writer – and 'The Timber Man'.

'The Timber Man' is an old song about a logger, while 'Tiger Whitehead' tells the story of a famous hunter. The most touching song on this album is the classic 'Old Shep', which Cash performs with just his guitar.

Johnny Cash wrote all of the songs on *Ragged Old Flag*, which came out in 1974. The album came at a time when America was getting out of Vietnam, only to become embroiled in the Watergate scandal of President Richard Nixon. The issues of Vietnam and Watergate would create a climate of distrust in the United States that would be felt heavily by the next generation and created a feeling of shame in the country. So when Johnny Cash recorded 'Ragged Old Flag', he confronted that sense of shame and countered with an unabashedly patriotic song.

Like so many of Cash's songs, this one tells a story. In this story, someone visits a small town and makes a derogatory comment about the torn and tattered flag in the square; an old man explains why the flag is torn and tattered – citing wars and triumphs – and concludes that the people are mighty proud of that 'ragged old flag' for having come through the fire.

On the liner notes to this album Cash writes that 'Ragged Old Flag' 'came out faster than I could write it down. It was a song that I didn't even have any control over.' For the rest of the songs on the album Cash states:

It seemed like in the last year or two, these songs started bubbling out of me more than ever and I started putting down everything that came out. I sang them for my family and my friends, and all they had to do was say they liked one and I'd go write another one. I've been doing things I did twenty years ago, jumping up in the middle of the night, grabbing a piece of paper in the dark, writing down a line or two so I wouldn't forget it tomorrow, and I found myself actually finishing all the songs that I started. It was like I was about to audition my own songs for the first time and I'd grab every passing thought, every catchy phrase and put it down. And there were times I even took my guitar to the supper table. I was working so hard on a song, I didn't want to give it up even for a few minutes. So while I ate with my family, I worked on the song at the same time and they cut my songs to pieces. I have an understanding with my wife and girls. They shoot straight with me on what they like and what

43

they don't like concerning my songs.

Cash said of these songs, 'Some of them came easy, within a matter of minutes or an hour at the most. But on some of them, I wrung my mind. I bit the pen and I walked the floor and the songs didn't want to come . . . I guess you'd say they are some of my most profound, passing thoughts.'

'Don't Go Near the Water' is an environmental song about the pollution of water and how that affects a father fishing with his son; 'All I Do Is Drive' is a song about truck drivers and counters the idea of the romance of the road with the reality that all he does is drive. 'Southern Comfort' is about someone who makes snuff from tobacco with the brand name 'Southern Comfort', but which provides no comfort at all while he's working. 'King of the Hill' is about ambition – and how it frustrates the life of a cotton-mill worker. 'Pie in the Sky' is a song about the afterlife in heaven, after the trials and turmoil of life on earth.

'Lonesome to the Bone' is about facing a morning with a hangover and without love; 'While I've Got It On My Mind' is about life at home and having the urge for sex and wanting it fulfilled. 'Good Morning Friend' is a gospel song about the joys of being born again. 'I'm a Worried Man' is the story of a man who's been fired from his job with a family to feed. 'Please Don't Let Me Out' is the story of a prisoner who's being paroled, but who is not comfortable in the 'free' world so he begs to be kept in prison. 'What On Earth (Will You Do for Heaven's Sake)' is a chastisement of religious people who have no pragmatism in their faith.

Cash's album *The Junkie and the Juicehead Minus Me* featured some of his family members. On this album, 'I Do Believe' and 'Bill and Rex and Oral and Bob' were written by Cash. 'Billy and Rex and Oral and Bob' is a tribute to (mostly) television preachers. This album was followed by a collection of old hymns, *Precious Memories*, and then *John R. Cash*, which had only 'Lonesome to the Bone' (previously released on *Ragged Old Flag*), which he wrote.

'Strawberry Cake' was performed by Cash at The Grand Ole Opry on 14 July 1975, during a benefit performance for multiple sclerosis.

It was also recorded live at the Palladium in London, England, in September. This concert was edited and released on the album *Strawberry Cake*. Other Cash songs on this album include 'Navajo', a tribute to the Southwestern Indian tribe, and 'Destination Victoria Station', about the popular London station.

Cash's next major album was *One Piece At A Time*, which featured the hit single about a man stealing a car one piece at a time from a factory in order to build it at home. Cash's songs on this album were 'Let There Be Country' (written with Shel Silverstein), 'Mountain Lady', 'Michigan City Howdy-Do', 'Sold Out of Flagpoles', 'Committed to Parkview', 'Daughter of a Railroad Man' and 'Go On Blues'. These are all good, strong songs, with 'Let There Be Country' taking a look at country music of that time; 'Michigan City Howdy-Do' is about a prisoner getting out of prison when he's old; 'Sold Out of Flagpoles' is a sort of stream-of-consciousness song with humorous asides; 'Go On Blues' is a simple song reminiscent of the Memphis days; 'Daughter of a Railroad Man' is about a lady who likes to leave; 'Mountain Lady' is the story of a mother whose son has returned home; and 'Committed to Parkview' is an especially strong song about life in a mental hospital.

The album *The Last Gunfighter Ballad* features Cash's song 'City Jail', a story song about the singer hassling a waitress. She calls the police, who arrive and hit him, then haul him off to jail while the waitress tells her boyfriend – who has come to get her – 'Get me away from that horrible man, Harry.' 'Cindy, I Love You' was written for Cash's daughter; 'Ballad of Barbara' is a combination of two old songs, 'Streets of Baltimore' and the old folk ballad 'Barbara Allen'. In this song, a man gets out of the country and into the city, then finds he wants to return, but his wife wants to stay in the city. 'Ridin' on the Cotton Belt' is semi-autobiographical, telling the story of how Cash's father would catch trains for work and then come back home.

The Rambler, recorded in early 1977, is an ambitious album. Cash has always had a fascination with motion, the idea of travelling and picking up adventures along the way. In a sense, travelling itself is a collection of experiences that are translated into songs, stories and accomplishments. His songs have often reflected this idea of the 'rambler', and this is part of his constant search for action to stimulate him. This album has Cash driving a car coast-to-coast, with dialogue interspersed. The dialogue comes with a hitchhiker Cash has picked up and the plot – a very loose one – involves him running into a girl along the way who has the same kind of wanderlust he does.

The songs are all written by Cash and the album begins with 'Hit the Road and Go', a song about a man leaving home because 'something was as wrong as if the sun forgot to rise', so he heads out to the Interstate where 'the rambler has cut all the ties and pulled up stakes to hit the road and go'. Next, the rambler picks up a young man who'd been fishing. The song 'If It Wasn't for the Wabash River' follows. In this song, the singer reflects that if it wasn't for the Wabash River, 'I'd be goin' crazy as an Indiana cyclone'. Next is 'Lady', a tender song where he remembers a woman whose 'arms were always warm and your bed was always ready'. He realises he loves her 'even more than I ever let you realise', and wants to tell her more but somehow 'can't find the way to write it down'.

'After the Ball', a rollicking song, follows where the rambler sings about waiting up for a woman so that when she finishes partying 'if you cannot stand, I've got a place for you to fall'. Gospel message follows with 'No Earthly Good', where the rambler chastises religious people whose faith avoids the practical. This is followed by a humorous song, 'A Wednesday Car', which harkens back to Cash's days on an automobile assembly line in Pontiac, Michigan. In this song, he informs his riders that only cars made on Wednesdays are any good because that's when auto workers are 'feelin' fine again and they're workin' like a dog and diggin' in/Tryin' to do everything they should'. The rest of the week is either looking forward to the weekend or recovering from it.

The female hitchhiker he picks up laments her lover is 'out on the range' and the rambler sings the song 'My Cowboy's Last Ride', about a man 'chasin' some stray'. Finally, she decides that 'a filly should be free for horsin' around', and so she 'will no longer be hobbled and tied'. The album concludes with 'Calilou', the name of a woman the rambler is looking for. He recounts how he met her while she was a waitress and then tried to settle down with her, but when he 'whispered words like "settle down" and "family"' she left. He admits that she should have been called 'trouble instead of Calilou'.

There were no hit singles from this album, although 'Lady' and 'After the Ball' both reached the lower part of the charts.

Johnny Cash suffered a dry spell on country radio from 1973 – the year after 'A Thing Called Love', 'Kate', 'Oney' and 'Any Old Wind That Bows' had all come out – until 1976, when 'One Piece at a Time' reached number one. Then, after 'One Piece at a Time', there was another dry spell until 1979, when 'Ghost Riders in the Sky' reached the number-two position on *Billboard*'s charts. Still, he continued to record, put out albums and tour. But the country music world was caught up in 'outlaws' and enamoured with Waylon and Willie. Ironically, after his TV show and patriotic songs, Johnny Cash was too much of an establishment figure by this time to benefit from this 'outlaw movement' of the late 1970s, although he recorded a hit single with Waylon Jennings, 'There Ain't No Good Chain Gang'. Another creative high point during the 1980s was his involvement in The Highwaymen, a group consisting of Cash, Waylon Jennings, Willie Nelson and Kris Kristofferson.

On the album *I Would Like to See You Again*, Cash seems to look back and re-examine parts of his life, concluding that he likes it where he's at. On 'I'm Alright Now', he sings about being a 'rambler', a 'gambler', and in trouble, 'ridin' on the devil's train' and 'in jail pretty close to hell', but is glad he is now walking with the Lord. On 'Lately', the singer examines his lover and sees 'the writing on the wall' that she'll soon leave. He notes she will 'look through me as if I'm another man/Instead of [her] own one and only', before concluding that, 'Things have not been working for us lately.' In 'Who's Gene Autry?', a tender, loving song, Cash tells of his young son climbing on his lap as a Gene Autry movie comes on TV and asking, 'Who's Gene Autry?' This allows Cash to relate how important Gene Autry was to his own boyhood and encourages his own son 'to go ahead and watch the show/And then ride off into the sunset with him like I did forty years ago'.

'Abner Brown' is the story about the town drunk where the singer grew up. But though Abner is a bum to the 'fine fancy people' who 'tolerated him', he was a hero to the kids 'cause he told us tales till our eyes grew wide'. The singer remembers Abner with fond memories and prays, 'Lord, take me back to the cotton land/ To Arkansas . . ./Let me be the boy that I once have been', because 'I still like to sit me down/Talk to my old friend Abner Brown.'

There are two songs written by Cash on his album *Gone Girl*: 'It Comes and Goes' and 'I Will Rock and Roll With You'. Both seem to look back at his Memphis roots while examining his life with June. The album *Silver* was done in 1980 to commemorate his twenty-fifth year in the music business. The songs he penned on that album were 'Lonesome to the Bone', which he recorded earlier; 'I'll Say It's True', which seeks to set the record straight about himself and June; and the revealing 'I'm Gonna Sit on the Porch and Pick on My Old Guitar'. Cash wrote this song when he was at his farm in Bon Aqua, Tennessee, just outside Nashville, drained and tired of the commitments and obligations he faced in his life. In this song, he yearns for the simple life of picking his guitar on the front porch and to 'fly away and never come back some day'. He wonders if anyone would miss him but then cautions, 'when my obligations load is a greasy uphill road/And pleasin' everybody but me is my first goal' whether he shouldn't just stay home.

The 1980s began on a high note for Johnny Cash; in October 1980 he was elected to the Country Music Hall of Fame. During the 1980s Cash left Columbia Records and recorded for a variety of labels and sang on a number of other artists' recordings. He continued to tour, appeared in several TV movies, as well as on some TV series, such as *Dr Quinn, Medicine Woman*. He also wrote a novel, *Man in White*. Perhaps the most self-satisfying work for Cash during the very early 1980s was his double album of gospel songs, *A Believer Sings the Truth*, recorded for the Cachet label. On this album, Cash was able to express the many dimensions of his faith. There is an old hymn ('Oh Come, Angel Band'), an old southern gospel favourite ('Gospel

Boogie'), some spirited black gospel ('There Are Strange Things Happening Everyday') and a spiritual ('Children Go Where I Send Thee'). He also wrote a number of songs for this album.

In his gospel songs, Cash's early work shows him repeating themes he'd heard in church or retelling biblical stories. But by the time of this album he was trying to apply the gospel message to the contemporary world and find new insights into biblical messages. 'Wings in the Morning' is reminiscent of his early work, as he sings about life after death; 'When He Comes' tells of the Second Coming. 'I'm a Newborn Man' was co-written with his young son, John Carter, and came from a phrase the young boy was singing. 'I'm Gonna Try to Be That Way' was recorded previously and talks of his commitment to be like Jesus. 'What on Earth (Will You Do For Heaven's Sake)' is an admonishment to believers to live the Christian life here on earth, while 'Over the Next Hill' is about the coming end times.

The most interesting songs on the album are 'The Greatest Cowboy of Them All' and 'You'll Get Yours and I'll Get Mine'. In the first song, he compares Jesus to his cowboy heroes and uses cowboy imagery to point out that Jesus 'loves all his little dogies' and that 'he'll lift up any maverick that falls/He loves every stray that scatters'. Cash concludes that Jesus 'will take us through the wire/Right on to that plain that's higher' because 'he's the greatest cowboy of them all'. On 'You'll Get Yours and I'll Get Mine', Cash states, 'I put everything on Jesus Christ and I'm gonna go for broke,' then admonishes listeners to 'live your time/Someday we'll all stand in line/When rewards are handed out/You'll get yours and I'll get mine.' Lest he appear judgmental, Cash's last verse states, 'what works for me don't necessarily mean it'll work for you/But I've tasted and I've tested and I know He's tried and true.'

This album seems to sum up Cash's spiritual life and spiritual journey better than any other. If he had never made another gospel album, this one would stand as an excellent summation of Cash's Christian beliefs.

But Cash did record another gospel album, *Believe in Him*, which was released in 1985. New Cash songs on this album include 'My

Children Walk in Truth', where he tells of the joy of his children being believers, and 'Half a Mile a Day', an excellent story song where an elderly lady stands up in church and tells of the struggles of the Christian life. It serves as a nice antidote to the fast-paced world of hurry-up-and-go we all live in. Cash's message is that Christianity is a long, slow walk if it's done right. On 'One of These Days I'm Gonna Sit Down and Talk to Paul', Cash expresses his desire to have a conversation with the biblical Paul so he can ask questions that have been burning for years. The Apostle Paul has intrigued Cash for years and was the subject of his novel, *Man in White*.

Creatively, the 1980s were a long dry spell for Johnny Cash. The decade began with the 'urban cowboy' craze and then moved away from traditional country into a 'countrypolitan' sound and image before Randy Travis arrived with old-fashioned country music in 1985. It was a difficult time for a legend like Johnny Cash. Although he collected honours and awards and was seen as a 'senior spokesman' for country music, he didn't seem to have a spot in the contemporary country music world. The excitement of new audiences and big sales left some of the old-timers in the dust. For someone like Johnny Cash, it was a frustrating, disappointing period.

Still, he stayed in the arena. On *Rockabilly Blues*, he wrote 'Cold Lonesome Morning, 'W-O-M-A-N', 'Rockabilly Blues' and 'She's a Go-er', which all looked back to the Memphis days and rockabilly that and become so appealing to the young audiences who weren't even born when Cash was cutting his first records. His songs didn't get played on the radio much, and in 1987 he switched to Mercury Records, but there wasn't much commercial success there either.

Then, in 1994, he released the album *Cash: American Recordings* on the new American Recordings label, produced by alternative producer Rick Rubin. The album was done with just Cash and his guitar and summed up Cash's career pretty well. The first song, 'Delia's Gone', was originally recorded by Cash in 1961. There were folk songs ('Tennessee Stud' and 'Delia's Gone'), a humorous song ('The Man Who Couldn't Cry'), a cowboy song ('Oh Bury Me Not'),

50

a gospel song ('Why Me, Lord'), songs with a haunting personal vision ('The Beast in Me' and 'Bird on a Wire'), and four songs he wrote. The self-penned songs tell stories that encompass Cash's spiritual vision. There was nothing new on this album except the audience. Young people suddenly discovered Johnny Cash and found him both profound and 'cool'. It was a surprising rebirth for a man whose audience and fans now included people younger than some of his grandchildren.

'Let the Train Whistle Blow' is yet another song with the imagery of a train, this time to carry his memory when he's gone. 'Drive On' is a song looking back at the wounds of Vietnam, while 'Redemption' is a straightforward gospel song about the old-time religion and a sinner washed in the blood. 'Like a Soldier' is the best of Cash's songs on this album. In this song, he looks back over his life and sees 'hidden memories come stealin' from my mind' as he looks at 'the wild road I was ramblin'' and admits, 'a hundred times I should've died.' Still, he believes, 'it was a road I was meant to ride' and so he feels 'like a soldier gettin' over the war'. He reflects on 'nights I don't remember and pain that's been forgotten/And a lot of things I choose not to recall', but in the end is 'thankful for the journey and that I survived the battles/And that my spoils of victory is you'.

During the last fifteen years of Johnny Cash's life he lived in pain, a result of his years of drug dependency, open heart surgery, diabetes, a misdiagnosis of Shy-Drager Syndrome that required medication, a broken jaw, and failing eyesight. Cash published his second autobiography in 1997 and during the book tour received the diagnosis of the fatal neurological disease, Shy-Drager. He stopped touring but continued recording for Rick Rubin and American Recordings.

After *Cash: American Recordings*, three other 'American' albums followed. These albums validated Cash's status and stature as an American icon and gained him a new, young audience.

His final album, *The Man Comes Around*, contains fifteen songs. It begins with the Cash-penned title song that carries the gospel message. But there's a double meaning – 'the man' could also be read as Johnny Cash giving his final message while he was alive.

The song 'Hurt', originally by the group Nine Inch Nails, was filmed as a video and won a number of awards from both MTV and the Country Music Association, which tells you a whole lot about the timeless appeal of Johnny Cash. Also on this final album he recorded one of his old songs, 'Give My Love to Rose', a Hank Williams song, 'I'm So Lonesome I Could Cry', the old western song 'Streets of Laredo', a Beatles song, 'In My Life', a Simon and Garfunkel song, 'Bridge Over Troubled Waters', and the Roberta Flack hit 'The First Time Ever I Saw Your Face'.

In May 2003, June Carter Cash went into hospital for heart surgery and fell into a coma. She died on 15 May, a devastating loss for Johnny Cash. Within a week after her death, Cash contacted some friends because he wanted to record some more songs. During the four months between her death and his own, Cash recorded about fifty songs. In September, he was set to fly to Los Angeles to record some more songs with Rick Rubin, but failing health forced him to enter hospital, where he died on 12 September.

After his death, a five-CD set containing 100 out-takes from the previous decade of recording with Rubin was released. There are more songs Cash and Rubin recorded that have yet to be released.

It took a long hard life to write the songs that Johnny Cash wrote, and a good sweet life to sing them. Johnny Cash lived both. The songs he wrote reflect both the hardness and the sweetness of his life, the sinner and the saint, the success and the failures, the strengths and weaknesses, all wrapped up in the greatness that called itself Johnny Cash.

Bibliography

Brooks, Tim and Earle Marsh, *The Complete Directory To Prime Time Network TV Shows 1946–Present*, Ballantine Books, New York, 1988

Cash, Johnny, *Man in Black*, Zondervan, Grand Rapids, MI, 1975

Cash, Johnny with Patrick Carr, *Cash: The Autobiography*, HarperSanFrancisco, New York, 1997

Smith, John L., *The Johnny Cash Discography*, Greenwood Press, Westport, CT, 1985

Whitburn, Joel, *Top Country Singles 1944–1988*, Record Research Inc., Menomonee Falls, WI, 1989

Wren, Christopher S., *Winners Got Scars Too: The Life and Legends of Johnny Cash*, The Dial Press, New York, 1971

MY FRIEND, THE FAMOUS PERSON
by Jack H. Clement

My friend, the famous person
Is a barrel full of fun
    A rather shy guy
    A very nice guy
In spite of all he's done

He's been around
This friend of mine
    Ten times ten
    And then again

    Down the river
    'Round the world
And up the creek times ten
But always springing forth and back again

For springing back
Brings secret laughter
And toughens up the chinny-chin
And lets the player fall down harder
    Just to get to bat again

To really know a fellow person
Takes a while, you know
    It's seldom easy
    But easily worth it
Just to find a kindred soul

A kindred soul will pass the test
Or flunk it just for spite
Just to enjoy being a human
    So let him do it

It's his right
Scold him quickly if he needs it
And never be a yesing man
    Tell him no
    When no's the answer
Or a lie he'll love and understand

A kindred soul comes back around
And never really leaves
Though some time may pass
While he seems like an ass
He'll show up in one of your dreams

Just to enjoy being a human
    So let him do it
    It's his right

My friend, the famous person
Is a pal you might know, too
For he has a lot of friends
And that's what makes him true

And true finds truth to realize
That there's more to truth
    Than the absence of lies

It takes a good man to take success
    And not misplace his soul
Though bumbling through the facts of life
    And too much rock and roll

He's a hero still drifting backward
Ever rising from the South
    Ever learning
    Ever earning
My attention span

MY FRIEND, THE FAMOUS PERSON

He gives a lot, this friend of mine
He lives a lot, this friend of mine
    And loves from way within
    And defeats the lust for anger
Whether he needs it or not
Just to enjoy being a human

But never guilt should my friend feel
That's neither good nor dignified
    It's negative
    Wrong
And an all-round bad deal

    For fame's a law
    And love's a duty
And that could put one on the fence
But laughter loose and silly-hearted
Makes it all make sense

GOD

LEAD ME FATHER
(originally titled 'My Prayer')

When my hands get tired,
When my steps get slow,
Walk beside me and give me
    The strength to go
Fill my face with Your courage,
So defeat won't show
And pick me up when I stumble,
    So the world won't know

Lead me, Father,
    With the staff of life,
And give me strength for a song
That the words I sing
Might more strength bring
To help some poor troubled weary worker along

When my way is clear,
And I fail to see,
With Thy strong hands
Strike out the blindness in me
Show me work that I should
    Carry on for Thee
Make my way straight and narrow
As You would have it be

IT WAS JESUS

Well, a man walked down by Galilee,
So the Holy Book does say.
And a great multitude was gathered there
Without a thing to eat for days.
Up stepped a little boy with a basket.
'Please take this, Lord,' he said.
And with just five loaves and two little fishes,
Five thousand had fish and bread
    Who was it, everybody?
    Who was it, everybody?
    Who was it, everybody?
It was Jesus Christ our Lord

Now, pay close attention, little children;
It's somebody you ought to know.
It's all about a man who walked on earth
Nearly two thousand years ago
Well, He healed the sick and afflicted,
And He raised them from the dead.
Then they nailed Him on an old rugged cross
And put thorns on His head

Well, they took him down and buried Him,
And after the third day,
When they came to His tomb, well,
They knew He was gone for the stone was rolled away.
'He's not here for He is risen,'
    The angel of the Lord did say.
And when they saw Him walking
With His nail-scarred hands they knew
He came back from the dead

LAND OF ISRAEL

From the top of Sinai to the Sea of Galilee,
  Ev'ry hill and plain is home,
  Ev'ry place is dear to me.
There the breezes tell the stories
Oh, what stories they do tell;
Of the mighty things that happened in the land of Israel

Hear when Moses and the prophets
  Spoke of one who would be king,
Of a heavenly Messiah
  And the blessings He would bring.
Oh, to hear again the call,
All is peaceful all is well,
Upon ev'ry rock and mountain in the land of Israel

From the rolling plain of Sharon
  To Mount Tabor's lofty heights,
To the desert of Beersheba,
All is calm, all is right.
Green the trees are on the mountain,
  Sweet water in the well;
May there never more be sorrow in the Land of Israel

BELSHAZZAR

Well, the Bible tells about a man
Who ruled Babylon and all its land
Around the city he built a wall
And declared that Babylon would never fall
He had concubines and wives
He called his Babylon paradise
Upon his throne he drank and ate
But for Belshazzar it was getting late

For he was weighed in the balance
    And found wanting
His kingdom was divided, couldn't stand
He was weighed in the balance
    And found wanting
His houses were built upon the sand

Well, the people feasted and drank the wine
And praised the false gods of his time
All holy things they scorned and mocked
Suddenly all their mocking stopped
On the wall there appeared a hand
Nothing else, there was no man
But the hand began to write
And Belshazzar couldn't hide his fright

Well, no one around could understand
What was written by the mystic hand
Belshazzar tried but he couldn't find
A man to give him peace of mind
Daniel the prophet a man of God
He saw the writing on the wall and looked
Belshazzar asked him what it said
And Daniel turned to the wall and read:
You are weighed in the balance

And found wanting
Your kingdom is divided, it can't stand
You are weighed in the balance
   And found wanting
Your houses are built upon the sand

MATTHEW 24
(Is Knocking at the Door)

I heard on the radio
There's rumors of war
People gettin' ready for battle
And there may be just one more

I heard about an earthquake
And the toll it took away
These are the signs of the times we're in today

Matthew 24 is knocking at the door
And there can't be too much more to come to pass

Matthew 24 is knocking at the door
And a day or one day more could be the last

The great bear from the northland
Has risen from his sleep
And the army ranks in red
Are near 200 million deep
The young and old now prophesy
A coming Prince of Peace
And last night I dreamed of lightning in the East

ANOTHER WIDE RIVER TO CROSS

I've stood on the bank by the weeping willow
  With another wide river to cross
  Another wide river to cross
  With another wide river to cross
And I believe I can make it to the other side
Cause I feel a hand on me
Helping me with
  Another wide river to cross

And I wake up to a many a day
  With another wide river to cross
  With another wide river to cross
  Another wide river to cross
I jump right into dark and swim right on
Toward the light on the other side
It's always there when there's
  Another wide river to cross

Oh, the whirlpools twist and pull at me
  With another wide river to cross
  Another wide river to cross
  With another wide river to cross
And if I reach up a hand is always reaching down for me
It's always there when there's
  Another wide river to cross

Well, the river Jordan is a narrow stream
  But it's another wide river to cross
  It's another wide river to cross
  It's another wide river to cross
But I believe there's a resting place
That's provided just for me
On the heaven side of
  Another wide river to cross

HALF A MILE A DAY

One night after a concert I walked through the streets of the town.
Passed a little church; the service was over but the testimonials
had just begun, and all caught up in the fervor and excitement of
the evening, I stepped in and sat down by a little lady in the
back.

A man at the front stood up and said, 'Preacher, I want you to know
I'm going to heaven just as fast as I can go, like an arrow shot from
a bow,' then he sat down.

Another man stood up and said, 'Preacher, I'm sailing into the
portals of heaven like a giant clipper ship right into your safe
blue harbor and nothing is going to deter me on the way,' and he
sat down.

Another man said, 'I'm sailing into heaven like a giant airplane on
silver wings landing on your golden shore by and by.'

Well, the little lady beside me waited until it all quieted down and
she made it to her feet and with her face turned not toward the
preacher nor the congregation but toward the Lord, she said:

I am coming, Lord, for my heavenly reward
I'm on my way to you
  Can't you see me coming through?
Through clouds of persecution
And I'm stumbling all the way
And with my mistakes I barely make
  A half a mile a day

But the road to heaven never had a rapid transit plan
It's one way with no changes
  Straight through to Promised Land
But I believe that if I need the words He had to say

Even I can get to heaven at
A half a mile a day

Lord, when I let you lead
I don't make any speed
Cause you have me stop and touch all
The ones that need so much
And then sometimes I get tempted
And I fall along the way
And with my mistakes I barely make
    A half a mile a day

And the whole congregation said, 'Amen, sister.'

MY CHILDREN WALK IN TRUTH

I pray to know more joy in my salvation
A selfish prayer I finally came to know
    For my greatest joy in living
    Comes to me when I am giving
Giving children bread of life and watch them grow

And my greatest joy is knowing
That my children walk in truth
And that they are giving you, Lord
Of their fire and strength of youth
Yes, I found the greatest joy in my salvation
Is knowing that my children walk in truth

It's hard to feed someone else when you're hungry
You can't teach if you don't understand
    And no one will follow you
    If you don't live it each day through
A frightened child won't hold a trembling hand

ONE OF THESE DAYS I'M GONNA SIT DOWN AND TALK TO PAUL

One of these days I'm gonna sit down and talk to Paul
One of these days I'm gonna sit down and talk to Paul
   I will ask him about his journeys
   And he will tell me about them all
One of these days I'm gonna sit down and talk to Paul

He will introduce me to Luke and Timothy
He will introduce me to Luke and Timothy
   I will be so glad to meet them
   And they'll be glad to meet me
He will introduce me to Luke and Timothy

I will ask him about that trip to Phillipi
How he and Silas felt at Phillipi
   At the miracle at Midnight
   When the jail doors opened wide
We'll sing those songs at Phillipi

I will ask him if he ever went to Spain
I will ask him if he ever went to Spain
   I'll find out if he made it
   I'll find out his secret pain
I'll ask him if he ever went to Spain

ALL OF GOD'S CHILDREN AIN'T FREE

I'd sing more about more of this land
But all God's children ain't free
I'd open up every door I can
Cause all God's children ain't free

I met a beaten, broken man
He shovels dirt but got no land
And he held out his hand to me
And all God's children ain't free

I'd sing along to a silly song
But all God's children ain't free
I'm gonna sing a blues
For the man they done wrong
Cause all God's children ain't free

Mister, how 'bout the man you condemned to die
By takin' everything that he's living by
And reject him from society
All God's children ain't free
No, reject him from society
All God's children ain't free

I'd be happy walking any street
But all God's children ain't free
I'd have a smile for all I meet
But all God's children ain't free

I'd whistle down the road
But I wouldn't feel right
I'd hear somebody cryin' out at night
From a sharecropper's shack or penitentiary
All God's children ain't free
From a sharecropper's shack or penitentiary
All God's children ain't free

NAZARENE

Caesar ruled Rome and all its glory
Every land called Alexander great
But no man can compare in any story
With the one man who controlled so many's fate

Yes, along the dusty road came the Nazarene
Baptized by John was the Nazarene
Preachin' on the top of the mountain was the Nazarene
Followed by the multitude was the Nazarene
   Tried and condemned
   They laid their stripes on him
But like he said
Back from the dead came the Nazarene

Nothing good had ever come from Nazareth
An unimportant place in Galilee
But the soul of any man could fall into bondage
And God had promised man could be set free

Then along the dusty road came the Nazarene

THE CHRISTMAS SPIRIT

RECITATION:

On Christmas Eve I dreamed I traveled all around the Earth
And in my dream I saw and heard the ways the different people
Hailed the king whose star shone in the East
    And what a dream it was
In London town I walked around Piccadilly Circus
A mass of people moving here and there
    I wondered where?
On every face at every place was
    Hurry up, I'm late!
But a kind old man at a chestnut stand
Said 'Merry Christmas, mate.'
    And I felt the Christmas spirit

In a little town nestled down in Bavaria, Germany
I walked along to see what the feeling there would be
And here again was the busy den
    The rushing, the yelling
But some kind voice said
'Frohliche Weihnachten'
Not understandin' the words
But forgettin' the buying and selling
    I felt the Christmas spirit

In Bethlehem I heard a hymn some distant choir sang
And with other tourists I walked along to a church
    As its bells rang
Then I heard someone tell someone
'There's where Christ was born!'
I wonder if He looked like our baby looked
On that first morn
And then I really felt the Christmas spirit

72

From a businessman in the Holy Land
    At a sidewalk souvenir shop
I bought a little Bible, since I'd already stopped
And it was in Paris, France, somehow by chance
That I took the Bible out and as I flipped the pages
I saw these words and I knew what it was all about
For I read
    'Fear not, for behold I bring you good tidings
    of great joy
    which shall be to all people
    for unto you is born this day
    in the city of David a Savior
    which is Christ the Lord.'

Then I took the little holy book
    Held it close and tight
I closed my eyes and visualized the glory of that night
So suddenly it came to me
For when I woke Christmas day
I felt the Christmas spirit
    Down deep inside to stay

THE GIFTS THEY GAVE

Jesus our king, kind and good
Was humbly born in a stable of wood
And the lowly beasts around Him stood
Jesus our king, kind and good

I, said the donkey, shaggy and brown
I carried His mother up and down
I carried His mother to Bethlehem town
I, said the donkey, shaggy and brown

I, said the ox, this was my hay
I gave Him my manger, t'was here that He lay
I gave Him my manger, t'was there that He lay
I, said the ox, this was my hay

I, said the sheep with curly horn
I gave Him my wool, a blanket warm
He wore my coat on Christmas morn
I, said the sheep with curly horn

I, said the dove from the rafters high
I sang Him to sleep so that He would not cry
We sang Him to sleep, my love and I
I, said the dove from the rafters high

And so every heart by some good spell
In the stable dark was glad to tell
Of the gift that he gave to Emmanuel
Of the gift that he gave to Emmanuel

WE ARE THE SHEPHERDS

So here is the stable and there is the manger
The new Savior sleeps on His first earthly night
    The wise men brought riches
    But we brought a candle
It's all that we have but it gives a good light

We are the shepherds
We walked 'cross the mountains
We left our flocks when the new star appeared
Oh, the beautiful singing of heavenly choirs
    We had to come see Him
    We had to come here

We beg you forgive us
For such a small offering
But our sheep are out there
With wolves in the night
We bring you this candle
'Tis all we have with us
But with it the new Savior
    Has His first light

We thank thee, kind Joseph
For bidding us enter
Please take our gift
    For the new babe of thine
'Tis only one candle
But it is our symbol
Of how we believe
    His great light will shine

WHO KEPT THE SHEEP?
(with Ezra Carter)

The shepherds afar left their flocks by night
Followed the new star by its heavenly light
    Did the lambs fear the wolves?
    Did they lay down and sleep?
Who kept the sheep?
Who kept the sheep?

Did robbers not steal or did they fear the light?
That the shepherds had followed night after night
    Did they not stray?
    Did little lambs weep?
Who kept the sheep?
Who kept the sheep?

Under the new star, the new Savior lay
In His little manger, He lay on the hay
    The shepherds that came
    Had a vigil to keep
But who kept the sheep?
Who kept the sheep?

Who kept the sheep?
Who kept the sheep?

I'M GONNA TRY TO BE THAT WAY

Once upon a lifetime there lived a man, um um
Many years ago in a foreign land
   Knew how to live right,
   Tried to be a light
Gave everybody a helping hand

I'm gonna try to be that way, um um
I'm gonna try to be that way
   Do the kind of things a man oughta do
   Say the kind of things a man oughta say
I'm gonna try to be that way

He never done anybody wrong, um um
He tried to help everybody 'long
   He brought a better land
   To make a better man
Out of the rich or the poor or the weak or the strong

And He preached love and brotherhood, uh huh
He went around doin' good, doin' good
   Everywhere He went
   They knew that He was sent
And the people started actin' like they should

GOD

HE'LL BE A FRIEND

Well, God told Noah to build an ark
He said it's gonna rain, gonna be dark
Call in the animals two by two
And don't let a sinful man go through

So the flood came just like He said
And every evil thing on earth was dead
But Noah's faith was like a rock
God laid his ark on a mountaintop

He'll be a friend and guide you
He'll walk along with you
You'll feel it there inside you
He'll help you make it through

When things looked dark Noah saw the light
Cause faith had told him right is might
If you need a friend He'll guide you
He'll be a friend to you

Well, you've heard of Samson the strong man
The mightiest man in all the land
There was one purpose for his might
He had to deliver the Israelites

By the Philistines he was overcome
They tied him up to carry him home
But Samson prayed and his bonds were gone
He killed a thousand with an old jawbone

He'll be a friend and guide you
He'll walk along with you
You'll feel it there inside you
He'll help you make it through

God showed Samson what to do
And it's the same God that stands by you
If you need a friend He'll guide you
He'll be a friend to you

I CALL HIM
(with R. Cash)

Well, the blue's still in the water
And the blue's still in the sky
And way beyond the blue there's someone
   Watchin' from on high
My clothes may be ragged and my shoes may be worn
But I've been a wealthy boy since I've been born

Cause I call Him when I'm troubled
And I call Him when I'm weak
And He always pulls me through my troubles some way

And I believe He'll be there,
   He'll be there
Like He always is to answer when I call Him

My mother used to tell me I should take it slow
The pace is not what matters
   It's the direction that you go
Keep your feet upon the path
And your eyes upon the goal
You'll have the joy a heart could ever hold

PRAISE THE LORD

The people that walked in the darkness
Have seen a great light
They that dwell in the land of shadow of death
Upon them had the light shined bright

For unto us a child is born
Unto us a son is given
And His name shall be called 'Wonderful'
The Prince of Peace to show the way to heaven

I SEE MEN WALKING AS TREES

Jesus came to the city of Bethsaida
And the blind man was brought to him
And the blind man said to Jesus

If you'd only stop and touch me
If you'd only stop and touch me
If you'd only stop and touch me
    I know I could see

If you'd only stop and touch me
If you'd only stop and touch me
If you'd only stop and touch me
    I know I could see

So Jesus touched him
He put his hands on the blind man's eyes
    And He said
'Now, open your eyes and tell me what you see'
And I can almost see that man now opening his eyes
    For the first time
Looking around and seeing the dim outline
    Of the people around him

He said:

I see men as trees walking
I see men as trees walking
I see men as trees walking
    I'm beginning to see

I see men as trees walking
I see men as trees walking
I see men as trees walking
    I'm beginning to see

JOHNNY CASH THE SONGS

So Jesus touched him one more time
He laid His hands on his eyes and said,
'Now open your eyes
And look up and tell me what you see'
And the man said:

I can see all men clearly
I can see all men clearly
I can see all men clearly
  I've begun to see

I can see all men clearly
I can see all men clearly
I can see all men clearly
  I've begun to see

And if all that be true
Then I've just got one more thing to say:

Jesus reach down now and touch me
Jesus reach down now and touch me
Jesus reach down now and touch me
  I would like to see

Jesus reach down now and touch me
Jesus reach down now and touch me
Jesus reach down now and touch me
  I would like to see

JESUS WAS A CARPENTER

Jesus was a carpenter
And He worked with a saw and a hammer
And His hands could form a table
True enough to stand forever

And He could have lived his life out
In the little town of Nazareth
But He put aside His tools
And He walked the burning highways
And to certain people He said, 'Follow me'

And He found them as He wandered
Through the wild Judean mountains
And He found them as they pulled their nets
Upon the Sea of Galilee

And for a thousand evenings
As the day behind Him emptied
He walked among the poor
And He stopped to touch the dying
And He built His house for folks like you and me

Would He stand today upon the sands of California
And walk the sweating blacktop in New York or Mississippi
    Where the mighty churches rise up
    High above the screaming cities
Could He walk among us with no ridicule or hatred
Would He be a guest on Sunday
A vagrant on a Monday
Would we lock our doors against His kind today?

Come again Lord Jesus
Be a carpenter among us
There are chapels in our discontent
Cathedrals to our sorrow

And we live in golden mansions
With the sand for our foundations
   And the raging waters rising
   And the thunder's all around us
   And the trouble's all around us
Won't you come and build a house on rock again?

CHRISTMAS WITH YOU

It's so nice to spend Christmas with you
The times that I've seen Christmas come and go
    Are now two score
I wish you Merry Christmas
And I wish you many more
It's good to see the children laugh with joy
    The way they do
And it's nice to spend Christmas with you

That old-fashioned Christmas
    Is a sweet memory
Except for all the Christmases
That you weren't there with me
But I really feel the spirit
Cause I love you like I do
And it's nice to spend Christmas with you

I remember Christmas
When I little could afford
And I tried to remember
It's the birthday of our Lord
    Well, I'll not forget to thank Him
    For His blessings on we two
And that I can spend Christmas with you

WHEN HE COMES

Every eye shall see
Every ear shall hear
The sound of angels
   When He comes
   When He comes

Every knee shall bow
Every tongue shall confess
That He is Lord
   When He comes
   When He comes

And He'll plant his beautiful feet
Upon this mountain
And the dead of all the ages
Who believed on Him will rise
   And I'll be one
   I'll be one
In the first resurrection
   When He comes
   When He comes
   When He comes

Every one then will know
That it's Him, really Him
The one and only
   When He comes
   When He comes

Glorified and transformed
I'll raise at his call
I'll be ready
   When He comes
   When He comes

I'M A NEWBORN MAN
(with J.C. Cash)

I'm a newborn man
I'm a newborn man
I'm a newborn man
And on a rock I stand
I'm a newborn man

He put a light on me
He put a light on me
He put a light on me
So now I can see
He put a light on me

He loves me all the time
Loves me all the time
He loves me all the good time
I'm His and He's mine
He loves me all the time

I was dying and the time was flyin'
Then I heard Him callin' me
My will was bent, I did repent
And His sweet love set me free

I'm a newborn man
I'm a newborn man
I'm a newborn man
And on a rock I stand
I'm a newborn man

WINGS IN THE MORNING

Wings in the morning and license to fly
Straight to the portals of never more die
Never more pain in them ole achin' bones
Wings in the morning to carry us home

My grandfather lived by the Book all his life
On rich bottom land with twelve kids and a wife
He never saw TV nor rode a jet airplane
But he knew that heaven was holding his claim

The salt of the Earth yet with faith in the Lord
They all got together and that one accord
And what could be greater than God's guarantee
That we can have heaven for eternity

Rocks in the road and we stumble and fall
Light's gettin' low so we don't see at all
But I promise you on that gettin' up day
Wings in the morning and we'll fly away

OVER THE NEXT HILL

By the way the land is layin'
I think I'd be safe in sayin'
That over the next hill we'll be home
It's a straight and narrow highway
No detours and no byways
And over the next hill we'll be home

From the prophets I've been hearin'
I would say the end is nearin'
For I see familiar landmarks all alone
By the dreams that I been dreamin'
There will come a great redeemin'
And over the next hill we'll be home

By the turn the tide has taken
I would say there's no mistakin'
That over the next hill we'll be home
There's a place that we are nearin'
That so many have been fearin'
And over the next hill we'll be home

When we get there we're all hopin'
That we'll find the gate is open
And there'll be a refuge from the comin' storm
For the way's been long and weary
But at last the end is nearin'
And over the next hill we'll be home

WHAT ON EARTH WILL YOU DO
(For Heaven's Sake)

Would you walk that second mile?
Turn a frown with a smile?
Would you give a little more than you could take?
Did you shine your little light
Upon the children of the night?
What on earth will you do for heaven's sake?

Did you feed the poor in spirit?
And befriend the persecuted?
Did you show the bound
   How all the chains can break?
Did you sow the proper seed?
Do you walk among the weeds?
What on earth will you do for heaven's sake?

Are you patient with the weak?
Are you counted with the meek?
Would you lift a lowly heart
   Or let it break?
Could you give away your shirt?
And overlook a beggar's dirt?
What on earth will you do for heaven's sake?

THE GREATEST COWBOY OF THEM ALL

I've always had my heroes
I've loved a lot of legends
Many men in my mind are ridin' tall
But my cowboy hero hat's off
To the man who rode the donkey
He's the greatest cowboy of 'em all

He loves all His little dogies
He speaks to them kind and gently
And He'll lift up any maverick that falls
He loves every stray that scatters
Like he's the only one that matters
He's the greatest cowboy of them all

Once He rode into the sunset
But some returning sunrise
He'll call up all the riders in the sky
Gotta get my row together
Gettin' ready for that sunrise
That winds up where old cowboys never die

The trail He rides is narrow
But it's straighter than an arrow
And He rides point for all the great and small
He will take us through the wire
Right on to that plain that's higher
He's the greatest cowboy of them all

WELCOME BACK JESUS

Lord, if You should be
Lookin' down at little me
   I'd just like to say
   I'm trying to stay
Upon the right track

But Lord, the way gets hard
Temptations come and I sure get tired
   But I'm watchin' for You
   Like You told me to
And welcome back

Welcome back Jesus
Welcome back Jesus
I'm watchin' for Your light to shine
Like You said it would shine
   When You come
Welcome back Jesus
Welcome back Jesus
I hope You will see
And recognize me
   And then take me home

THE PREACHER SAID, 'JESUS SAID'

Well, with everybody tryin' to tell us what to do
You wonder how you are to know whose word is true
But the preacher keeps on a-bringin' us the very same word
And from St Paul to Billy Graham the same is heard

And the preacher said of truth, 'Jesus said'

And Jesus said, 'I am the way, the truth and the life'

Well, we can see the world is full of greed
There's so much hate yet there is so much need
What should we do when no one seems to care
What can we do when there is no love there

And then the preacher said of love, 'Jesus said'

Jesus said, 'Love thy neighbour as thyself'

Well, please tell us the road we oughta go
In such confusion how are we to know
And if there is a heaven show us too its gaze
Ah, you better tell us preacher before it's too late

And then the preacher said of heaven, 'Jesus said'

Jesus said, 'Seek ye first the kingdom of God and his righteousness
    and all these things shall be added unto you.'

Well, please tell us how we can find the way
To climb to every mountain that we face every day
And in time of troubles what to depend upon
To be the truth and help us carry on
And the preacher said of trouble, 'Jesus said'

Jesus said, 'Let not your heart be troubled. If you believe in God, believe also in me. In my father's house are many mansions, if it were not so I would have told you. I go to prepare a place for you. And if I prepare a place for you, I will come again and receive you unto myself that where I am you may be also.'

COME TO THE WAILING WALL

Oh, my Lord, what a mornin'
Oh, my Lord, what a day
The sound of battle's over
And the smoke has blown away

Come to the Wailing Wall
Come to the Wailing Wall
Thank God you can stand
   Upon this Holy Land,
And touch the hallowed rock
That God delivered to our hand.
Come to the Wailing Wall;
Come to the Wailing Wall

Shout it 'cross the mountain,
Shout it 'cross the sea
We have been delivered,
   Israel is free

Bring the lost ones homeward,
Lead them to this shore
The city gates are open,
   Heaven's blessings pour

HE TURNED THE WATER INTO WINE

He turned the water into wine
   (Didn't my Lord, now),
He turned the water into wine.
   In the little Canaan town
   The word went all around
That He turned the water into wine

Well, He walked upon the Sea of Galilee;
He walked upon the Sea of Galilee
   Shouted far and wide,
   He calmed the raging tide,
And walked upon the Sea of Galilee

He healed the leper and the lame;
He healed the leper and the lame.
   He said, 'Go and tell no man,'
   But they shouted it through the land,
That He healed the leper and the lame.

He fed the hungry multitude;
He fed the hungry multitude,
   With a little bit of fish and bread,
   They said everyone was fed;
He fed the hungry multitude.

GOD IS NOT DEAD

When Jesus called to God upon the Cross;
No answer came, for His will must be done.
Then, how the world trembled at His voice,
When He said, 'This is my beloved Son'

It isn't God, but man's that dead
When love is locked outside.
Do you deny that there's a God,
Or is God just denied?
God is not dead;
He never died

What man on earth can make one blade of grass?
And who can make one seed, then make it grow?
With all the power and wisdom in our hands,
Who can command which way the wind to blow?
And who can match the miracle in an eagle's eye,
Or hang a rainbow in a cloudy sky?

God is not dead;
He did not die,
God is not dead;
God is not dead

BEAUTIFUL WORDS

Beautiful words,
Beautiful words
He spoke beautiful words
The wind lay still,
And the whole world listened
As He spoke beautiful words

NO EARTHLY GOOD

Come hear me, good brothers
Come heed one and all
Don't brag about standin'
Or you'll surely fall
Your shinin' your light
And shine it you should
But you're so heavenly minded
   You're no earthly good

No earthly good
You are no earthly good
You're so heavenly minded
   You're no earthly good
Your shinin' your light
And shine it you should
But you're so heavenly minded
   You're no earthly good

Come hear me, good sisters
You salt of the earth
If your salt isn't salty
Then what is its worth?
You could give someone
A cool drink if you would
But you're so heavenly minded
   You're no earthly good

No earthly good
You are no earthly good
You're so heavenly minded
   You're no earthly good
You could give someone
A cool drink if you would
But you're so heavenly minded
   You're no earthly good

JOHNNY CASH THE SONGS

If you're holdin' heaven
Then spread it around
There are hungry hands
Reachin' up here from the ground
Move over and share
The high ground where you stood
So heavenly minded
   You're no earthly good

REDEMPTION

From the hands it came down
From the side it came down
From the feet it came down
And ran to the ground

Between heaven and hell
A teardrop fell
In the crimson dew
The tree of life grew

And the blood gave life
To the branches of the tree
And the blood was the price
That set the captives free

And the numbers that came
Through the fire and the flood
Clung to the tree
And were redeemed by the blood

From the tree streamed the light
That started the fight
Round the tree grew a vine
On whose fruit I could dine

My old friend Lucifer came
Fought to keep me in chains
But I saw through the tricks
Of six-sixty-six

From His hands it came down
From His side it came down
From the feet it came down
And ran to the ground

JOHNNY CASH THE SONGS

And the small inner voice
Said you do have a choice
The vine ingrafted me
And I clung to the tree

And the blood gave life
To the branches of thee tree
And the blood was the price
That set the captives free

And with the numbers that came
Through the fire and the flood
I clung to the tree
And was redeemed by the blood

BILLY & REX & ORAL & BOB

Ordained for proclaiming the gospel of Jesus
The great super preachers go crusadin' on
And the people all gather in big congregations
To hear of the Savior who came to atone

And they kneel at the altar and they walk away happy
Then the Devil starts gossip about money and sex
Makin' it hard on the good men of God
Like Billy and Bob and Oral and Rex

Ole Billy Sunday is dead and gone
Young Jim Robison is comin' on strong
And Billy and Rex and Oral and Bob
Are talkin' about Jesus and doin' their job

Millions of people tune in Katherine Khulman
And see her face shine with an unearthly light
Garner Ted warns of the world of tomorrow
But they criticize him and the Reverend Ike

Cause the Devil is after the great super preachers
He'll try to discredit the gospel they bring
But Billy and Rex and Oral and Bob
Hold to their commitment to Jesus the King

Ole Billy Sunday is dead and gone
Young Tommy Barnett is comin' on strong
Young Jimmy Snow is comin' on strong

YOU'LL GET YOURS AND I'LL GET MINE

Live your time, stand in line
You'll get yours and I'll get mine

I don't like the taste of whiskey
Nor the smell of musky breath
And when they pass around the rocket ships
I've learned to let 'em pass

I'm not gonna drift away on powder
Not gonna blow away on smoke
I put everything on Jesus Christ
And I'm gonna go for broke

So live your time, live your time
Someday we'll all stand in line
When rewards are handed out
You'll get yours and I'll get mine

But no honorable mentions
Will come straddlin' down the line
Live your time, stand in line
You'll get yours and I'll get mine

I'm not pointin' any fingers
I'm not tryin' to be your light
I'm just tryin' to say that I believe
I'm finally gettin' it right

But what works for me don't necessarily
Mean it'll work for you
But I've tasted and I've tested
And I know He's tried and true

FIELD OF DIAMONDS
(with J.W. Routh)

Field of diamonds in the sky
Worlds a-whirling right on by
Are you wonderin' who am I?
Field of diamonds in the sky

Are you stars shining in his crown?
Or someone whose life's sun's
Going down, down, down?

Field of diamonds in the sky
Silent beauty shining bright
Are you tears the angels cry?
Field of diamonds in the sky

Will I be a star in his crown
Or someone who's life's sun's
Going down, down, down?

Field of diamonds in the sky
With the nights passing by
I will touch you by and by
Field of diamonds in the sky

MEET ME IN HEAVEN

We saw houses falling from the sky
Where the mountains leaned down to the sand
We saw blackbirds circling round an old castle keep
As I stood on the cliff and held your hand

We walk troubles brooding windswept hills
And we loved and we laughed the pain away
At the end of the journey, when our last song is sung,
Will you meet me in heaven someday?

Can't be sure of how it's going to be
When we walk into the light across the bar
But I'll know you and you'll know me
Out there beyond the stars

We've seen the secret things revealed by God
And we heard what the angels had to say
Should you go first, or if you follow me,
Will you meet me in heaven someday?

Living in a mansion on the streets of gold
At the corner of Grace and Rapture Way
In sweet ecstasy while the ages roll
Will you meet me in heaven someday?

In sweet ecstasy while the ages roll
Will you meet me in heaven someday?

THE MAN COMES AROUND

SPOKEN:

> And I heard, as it were, the noise of thunder
> One of the four beasts saying 'come and see',
> And I saw and behold a white horse

There's a man going 'round taking names
And He decides who to free and who to blame
Everybody won't be treated all the same
There'll be a golden ladder reaching down
>   When the man comes around

The hairs on your arm will stand up
At the terror in each sip and in each sup
For you partake of that last offer cup
Or disappear into the Potter's Ground
>   When the man comes around

Hear the trumpets, hear the pipers
One hundred million angels singing
Multitudes are marching to the big kettle drum
Voices calling, voices crying
Some are born and some are dying
It's alpha and omega's kingdom come

And the whirlwind is in the thorn tree
The virgins are all trimming their wicks
The whirlwind is in the thorn tree
It's hard for thee to kick against the pricks

Till Armageddon no Shalom, no Shalome
Then the father hen will call his chickens home
The wise men will bow down before the throne
And at his feet will cast their golden crowns
>   When the man comes around

JOHNNY CASH THE SONGS

Whoever is unjust, let him be unjust still
Whoever is righteous, let him be righteous still
Whoever is filthy, let him be filthy still
Listen to the words long-written down
    When the man comes around

In measured hundred-weight and penny-pound
    When the man comes around

SPOKEN:
    And I heard a voice in the midst of the four beasts
    And I looked and behold a pale horse
    And its name that set on him was Death
    And hell followed with him

COWBOYS, INDIANS AND OUTLAWS

THE FLINT ARROWHEAD

RECITATION:

Over fields of new-turned sod
And in communion with my God
   I walked alone
In a furrow bed I found an arrowhead
   Chiseled from stone
I don't know how long ago some red man drew his bow
   On its last flight
Or did he drop it here
Afraid white men were near
   To attack at night?

I do know this one thing beyond all questioning
   'Twas made to kill
And proof of a master trade
Is in this arrowhead he made
   Fashioned with skill
That I inherited this ground is denied
By this stone that I found
   But when and by who?

Come join me in my tracks
Then let's stop and look back
   To the veil and through
In love and peace we'll see
The shadows and the trees
   And voices too
But quietly slowly tread
This home of the forgotten dead
   Whose bones are dust
I'm proud that their craftsman's skill
Survives the ages still
   Left in my trust

COWBOYS, INDIANS AND OUTLAWS

DON'T TAKE YOUR GUNS TO TOWN

A young cowboy named Billy Joe grew restless on the farm
A boy filled with wanderlust, who really meant no harm
He changed his clothes and shined his boots
　　And combed his dark hair down
And his mother cried as he walked out:
　　'Don't take your guns to town, son;
　　Leave your guns at home, Bill;
　　Don't take your guns to town.'

He laughed and kissed his mom and said:
　　'Your Billy Joe's a man.
I can shoot as quick and straight as anybody can.
But I wouldn't shoot without a cause;
　　I'd gun nobody down.'
But she cried again as he rode away:
　　'Don't take your guns to town, son;
　　Leave your guns at home, Bill;
　　Don't take your guns to town.'

He sang a song as on he rode, his guns hung at his hips.
He rode into a cattle town, a smile upon his lips.
He stopped and walked into a bar and laid his money down,
But his mother's words echoed again:
　　'Don't take your guns to town, son;
　　Leave your guns at home, Bill;
　　Don't take your guns to town.'

He drank his first strong liquor then
　　To calm his shaking hand,
And tried to tell himself at last he had become a man.
A dusty cowpoke at his side began to laugh him down.
And he heard again his mother's words:
　　'Don't take your guns to town, son;
　　Leave your guns at home, Bill;
　　Don't take your guns to town.'

Bill was raged and Billy Joe reached for his gun to draw,
But the stranger drew his gun and fired before he even saw.
As Billy Joe fell to the floor the crowd all gathered 'round
And wondered at his final words:

    'Don't take your guns to town, son;
    Leave your guns at home, Bill;
    Don't take your guns to town.'

COWBOYS, INDIANS AND OUTLAWS

WHO'S GENE AUTRY?

Whoopee ti yi yo
Rocking to and fro
Back in the saddle again

My little boy said, 'Daddy, who's Gene Autry?'
His old movie was coming on TV
And I said, let me tell you about him, son
And I took him upon my knee
Why, when I was a little boy about your size
And just about every Saturday night
When I could scrape up a dime for the movies
And when my daddy said alright
I'd be right downtown at the picture show
Like everybody else that could
To see a handsome man on a big fine stallion
Going about doing good

Singing
   Whoopee ti yi yo
   Rocking to and fro
   Put him back in the saddle again
   Whoopee ti yi yay
   Let him go on his way
   Back in the saddle again

Why, he could ride his horse and play his guitar
And sing all at the same time
And I was riding right along there beside him
On that broomstick pony of mine
And you know, his pistol never ran out of bullets
When the bad guys had to be stopped
And somehow the bullets never drew any blood
But the bad guys dropped when he shot
Yeah, old Gene was the image of justice and goodness and purity

And in the eyes of a poor little country boy
He made the world look better to me

Singing
   Whoopee ti yi yo
   Rocking to and fro
   Put him back in the saddle again
   Whoopee ti yi yay
   Let him go on his way
   Back in the saddle again

And you know, the way he rescued the rancher's daughter
It sent a thrill right up the aisle
And the ending would always send us home
With a good victorious smile
Now you ask me, 'Who's Gene Autry?'
Well, son, go ahead and watch the show
And then ride off into the sunset with him
Like I did forty years ago

Singing
   Whoopee ti yi yo
   Rocking to and fro
   Put him back in the saddle again
   Whoopee ti yi yay
   Let him go on his way
   Back in the saddle again

COWBOYS, INDIANS AND OUTLAWS

HANK AND JOE AND ME

Well, in the desert where we searched for gold,
The days were hot, the nights were cold.
Hank and Joe and me walked on,
   So bold and brave and free
For days and days we fought the heat.
I got so thirsty and I got so weak.
And when I fell 'cause I couldn't go,
I heard Hank say to Joe,
   'He's dyin' for water.
   Hear him cryin' for water.'
Well, lay him down in the dust and sand
He said, 'Joe, you know he's a dyin' man.
Leave him there and let him die.
I can't stand to hear him cry for water.'

I don't remember how long I lay,
But when I awoke it was the break of day.
Buzzards circled miles ahead;
I knew Hank and Joe were dead,
My eyes were dimmed but I could see
A bed of gold nuggets under me.
Now I know that it won't be long
Till they decorate my bones.
   Cause I'm dyin' for water
   Can't help cryin' for water.

Well, they laid me down in the dust and sand
He said, 'Joe, you know he's a dyin' man.
Leave him there and let him die.
I can't stand to hear him cry for water.'
He couldn't stand to hear my cry for water.

YOU WILD COLORADO

Oh, you wild ragin' river
Like my woman's lips you lure me
Pied Piper of the desert
Roll on to the sea
You're the same at noon or midnight
And I'd follow where you go
But you're planning no returning
   You wild Colorado

If I had no love of life
I'd become part of your flow
But I fear the place you'd take me
   You wild Colorado

Oh, you wild ragin' river
From the fountains of the mountains
You ripple down the valleys
Growin' wide and swift and deep
With what power you cut your canyons
How long ago
You're as wayward as my woman
   You wild Colorado

MEAN AS HELL

The Devil in hell we're told was chained
A thousand years he there remained
He neither complained nor did he groan
But was determined to start a hell of his own

Where he could torment the souls of men
Without being chained in a prison bend
So he asked the Lord if He had on hand
Anything left when He made this land

The Lord said, 'Yes, there's plenty on hand
But I left it down by the Rio Grande
The fact is, old boy, the stuff is so poor
I don't think you could use it as a hell anymore.'

But the Devil went down to look at the truck
And said if he took it as a gift he was stuck
For after lookin' it over carefully and well
He said, 'This place is too dry for a hell.'

But in order to get it off His hand
The Lord promised the Devil to water the land
So a trade was closed and deed was given
And the Lord went back to his home in heaven
And the Devil, he said, 'Now I've got all that's needed
To make a good hell' and he succeeded

He began by putting thorns all over the trees
He mixed up the sand with millions of fleas
He scattered tarantulas along the road
Put thorns on cactus and horns on toads

Lengthened the horns of the Texas steer
Put an addition to the rabbit's ear

Put a little devil in the bronco's feed
And poisoned the feet of the centipede

The rattlesnake bites you, the scorpion stings
The mosquito delights you with his buzzing wings
The sand burrs are there and so are the ants
And if you sit down you'll need half soles on your pants
The wild boar roams on the black chaparral
It's a helluva place that he has for a hell

The heat in the summer is a hundred and ten
Too hot for the Devil, too hot for men
The red pepper grows upon the banks of the brook
The Mexicans use it in all that they cook
Just dine with one of 'em and you're bound to shout
I've hell on the inside as well as the out

My hands are calloused July to July
I use the Big Dipper to navigate by
Fight off the wolves to drink from my well
So I have to be mean as hell

A sheepherder came and put up a fence
I saw him one day but I ain't seen him since
But if you're needin' mutton we got mutton to sell
We're cow punchers and we're mean as hell

Neither me nor my pony's got a pedigree
But he takes me where I'm wantin' to be
I'll ride him to death and when he has fell
I'll get me another one, mean as hell

I shot me a calf and I cut off her head
Cause the boys in the bunkhouse were wantin' to be fed
They rise and shine with the 5.30 bell
And the best one of any of 'em is mean as hell

COWBOYS, INDIANS AND OUTLAWS

BIG FOOT

Big Foot was an Indian chief of the Miniconjou band
A band of Miniconjou Sioux from South Dakota land

Big Foot said to Custer, 'Stay away from Crazy Horse'
But Custer crossed into Sioux land
    And he never came back across
Then Big Foot led his people
To a place called Wounded Knee

And they found themselves surrounded
    By the Seventh Cavalry

Big Chief, Big Foot
Rise up from your bed
Miniconjou babies cry
For their mothers lying dead

Big Foot was down with the fever
When he reached Wounded Knee
And his people all were prisoners
    Of the Seventh Cavalry
Two hundred women and children
And another hundred men
Raised up a white flag of peace
    But peace did not begin

An accidental gunshot
And Big Foot was first to die
And over the noise of the rifles
You could hear the babies cry

Big Chief, Big Foot,
It's good that you can't see
Revenge is being wrought
By Custer's Seventh Cavalry

Then smoke hung over the canyon
On that cold December day
All was death and dying
Around where Big Foot lay
Farther on up the canyon
Some had tried to run and hide
But death showed no favorites
Women, men, and children died

One side called it a massacre
The other a victory
But the white flag is still waving
　　Today at Wounded Knee
Big Chief, Big Foot
Your Miniconjou band
Is mourned and remembered here
　　In South Dakota land

HIAWATHA'S VISION

On the shores of Gitachagoomee
By the shining big sea water
Hiawatha old and grey
Listened to the old prophet
 Listened to Yagoo
And the young men and the women from the land of Ojibways
From the land of the Dakotas, from the woodlands and the prairies

Stood and listened to the prophet
 Heard Yagoo tell Hiawatha

'I have seen,' he said
 'A water bigger than the big sea water
 Broader than the Gitchagoomee
 Bitter so that none could drink it
 Salty so that none would use it'

Hiawatha then spoke to them
Stopped all their jeering and their jesting
And he spoke to all the people
'It's true what Yagoo tells you
For I have seen it in a vision
I have also seen the water
To the east, to the land of morning
And upon this great water came a strange canoe with pinions
Bigger than a growth of pine trees
Taller than the tallest treetops
And upon this great canoe were sails to carry it swiftly
And it carried many people
Strange and foreign were these people
And white were all their faces
And with hair their chins were covered.'

'Then,' said Hiawatha
'I beheld the darker vision
Many hundreds came behind them
Pushed their way across our prairies
In our woodlands reigned their axes
In our valleys smoked their cities
Our people were all scattered,
    All forgetful of our councils
Left their homelands going westward wild and wilful
And the men with bearded faces
The men with skin so fair
With their barking sticks of thunder
Drove the remnants of our people
Further westward, westward, westward
Then wild, wild and wilder
Grew the west that once was ours.'

COWBOYS, INDIANS AND OUTLAWS

REFLECTIONS

Never in this world before
   Or nevermore hereafter
Could a land know such a people
As the pioneer, the cowboy
His clothes, his conversation
His unique brand of lingo
All his Devil deeds of daring
   His hat, his bandana
The dirty boots and ragged chaps
But mainly that six-gun dangling
So his hand could get it quickly

But draw your own conclusions
Lean to your own understandings
Your beliefs and your own convictions
   Disprove any fact recorded
In these sounds, and song and legends
   But I ask you if you do
Be sure you've walked in many moccasins
Over many, many pathways
And that you have listened carefully
Really listened to the west wind
And to everything it whispers
And then go back and listen
   Listen to this once more
To these legends and traditions
They're only one reflection
Of a tick of time, of that time
Just ponder on the things that happened ·
   As we gaze so very deeply
Into time and place and person
Seeing now and then the West as it really was
And to tell you of a little that we saw there
And looking backward through a century

That was the true West
There was the real true West
Not demanding an agreement
But rather helping you look with us
    And saw it as we saw it
And heard that west wind screaming, shouting
    Almost speaking
Always whispering of these things we sang and spoke of
And you'll hear perhaps the things
That we said in the stories
And the legends and traditions
Through the wind that breathed these tales
Of the ones who never made it
Yet fighting heat and mountains, plains and valleys
    Snow and hunger
They went westward, westward, westward

COWBOYS, INDIANS AND OUTLAWS

NED KELLY

Ned Kelly was a wild young bush ranger
Out of Victoria he rode with his brother Dan
He loved his people and he loved his freedom
And he loved to ride the wide open land

Ned Kelly was a victim of the changes
That came when his land was a-sproutin' seed
And the wrongs he did were multiplied in legend
With young Australia growin' like a weed

Ned Kelly took the blame
Ned Kelly won the fame
Ned Kelly brought the shame
And then Ned Kelly hanged

Well, he hid out in the bush and in the forest
And he loved to hear the wind blow in the trees
While the men behind the badge were comin' for him
Ned said they'll never bring me to my knees

But everything must change and run in cycles
And Ned knew that his day was at an end
He made a suit of armor out of plowshares
But Ned was brought down by the trooper's men

OLD APACHE SQUAW

Old Apache squaw
  How many long, lean years you saw?
  How many bitter winter nights
  Shiverin' in a cold tepee?
  Shiverin' in a cold tepee.

Old Apache squaw
  How many hungry kids you saw?
  How many bloody warriors
  Runnin' to the sea,
  Fleein' to the sea?
Well, now they tell me that you saw Cochise
When he made his last stand
He said,
  'The next white man what sees my face
  Is gonna be a dead white man.'

Old Apache squaw
  How many broken hearts you saw?
  You've had misty eyes for years
  Could that mist be tears?
  Could that mist be tears?

HARDIN WOULDN'T RUN

I know a man whose plow-handle hand
Is quicker than a light
Wes Hardin is his name, they say,
He travels in the night
    For he might have to kill
    Or walk around a fight

And if you ever saw Wes Hardin draw
You know he can skin his gun
He won't say how many tried and died
    Up against the top hand
    Up against the wrong man
Cause Hardin wouldn't run

He rode in like the Texas wind,
Took the Eastbound train
Goin', goin' with Jane Bowen,
Till the law men caught up
    'So long, Janie. Chin up.
    I'll be back again.'

Off he went to Huntsville prison
'So long, Jane,' he cried
Fifteen years she waited,
Till her heart broke and she died
    And she left that bad land
    To wait up in the sky

Free at last, the payin' past
For all the wrong he did
First free air they let him breathe
Since he was a kid
    So let him come and let him go,
    And let him deal and bid

JOHNNY CASH THE SONGS

Near the border in El Paso
'Lawyer' reads the sign
But you won't find him there
For bus'ness ev'ry day at nine
   For bus'ness is real bad,
   One client's all he had
   In quite a long time

Then Sheriff Selman's boy
Broke into Wes's woman's place
Up she jumped and pistol-whipped him,
Kicked him in the face
   And John Selman demands revenge
   For this disgrace

You can see her eve'ry night by candlelight
At Hardin's fav'rite bar
She'd be hangin' on his arm,
And very late they'd leave there
   Headin' for the goose hair,
   Glad it wasn't far

Through the swingin' door
John Selman came with blazin' gun
Wes Hardin chug-a-luggin' red eye,
Got him in the back of the head
   John Wesley Hardin fell dead,
   Cause Hardin wouldn't run

COWBOYS, INDIANS AND OUTLAWS

THE TALKING LEAVES

Sequoia's winters were sixteen;
Silent tongue – spirit clean
He walked at his father's side
Across the smoking battleground
Where red and white men lay around
So many men here had died.
The wind had scattered around
Snow white leaves upon the ground
Not leaves like leaves from trees.

Sequoia said:
    'What can this be?
    What's this strange thing here I see?
    From where come leaves like these?'

Sequoia turned to his father's eyes, and he said:
    'Father, you're wise.
    From where come such snow white leaves
    With such strange marks upon the squares?
    Not even the wise owl could put them there –
    So strange, these snow white leaves.'

His father, shielding his concern,
Resenting the knowledge Sequoia yearned,
Crumbled the snow white leaves.
He said:
    'When I explain, then it's done.
    These are talking leaves, my son.
    The white man's talking leaves.
    The white man takes a berry of black and red,
    And an eagle's feather from the eagle's bed
    And he makes bird track marks
    And the marks on the leaves, they say,
    Carry messages to his brother far away
    And his brother knows what's in his heart

They see these marks and they understand the truth
In the heart of the far-off man
The enemies can't bear them.'

Said Sequoia's father,
   'Son, they weave bad medicine on these talking leaves.
   Leave such things to them.'

Then, Sequoia, walking lightly,
Followed his father quietly.
But so amazed was he.
   If the white man talks on leaves,
   Why not the Cherokee?

Banished from his father's gaze,
Sequoia went from place to place.
   But he could not forget.
Year after year, he worked on and on.
Till finally he cut into stone the Cherokee alphabet.

Sequoia's hair, by now, was white.
His eyes began to lose their light.
But he taught all who would believe
That the Indian's thoughts could be written down.
And he left us these talking leaves.

TRAIL OF TEARS

There were many, many little children
Among the young and old who died
Up on the Trail of Tears
   Before they reached the other side

Sometimes at night I seem to hear a little Cherokee baby cry
And I seem to see campfires that burned for 10,000 years gone by;
And I heard a voice cry out these were our homes for all those years
And the trail that takes us away, will sure be a trail of tears

There were many, many little children
Among the young and old who died
Up on the Trail of Tears
   Before they reached the other side

The Cherokee looked up and saw that the autumn of their fate
Was burning bright upon the hills and their hour was getting late
And with the spring their smokes would here no longer touch the sky
Their lives here, like the last autumn leaves, would be a thing gone by

There were many, many little children
Among the young and old who died
Up on the Trail of Tears
   Before they reached the other side

The Cherokee who held on to their homes until the end
Asked to remain beside the whites who once had been their friend
Here the Cherokee Phoenix would no more touch the sky
Force upon a westward march thousands would die

There were many, many little children
Among the young and old who died
Up on the Trail of Tears
   Before they reached the other side

APACHE TEARS

Hoofprints and footprints
Deep ruts the wagons made,
The victor and the loser came by here
No headstones, but these bones
Bring mescalero death moans
See the smooth black nuggets
   By the thousands lying here
Petrified but justified
   Are these Apache tears

Dead grass, dry roots
Hunger cryin in the night
Ghost of broken hearts and laws are here
And who saw the young squaw,
They judged by their whiskey law
Tortured till she died of pain and tear

Where the soldiers lay her back
Are the black Apache tears

The young men, the old men
The guilty and the innocent,
Bled red blood and chilled alike with tears
The red man, the white man,
No fight ever took this land
So don't raise the dust
   When you pass here

They're sleeping in my keeping
   Are these Apache tears

COWBOYS, INDIANS AND OUTLAWS

MY COWBOY'S LAST RIDE

The cowboy's lady is cryin' tonight
Cause the cowboy's out on the range
Runnin' and ramblin' and chasin' some stray
And good cowboys don't ever change

I tried to hold him in the home corral
But the grasses were greener outside
So I'm gonna sit here in front of this door
   And I've loaded up my cowboy's .44
   When the smoke clears there'll be
    a new brand on his hide
This is my cowboy's last ride

Woo, woo, woo
I hate to see him go
But I won't be stayin' home cryin'
Ay ay ay
I hate to watch him die
But this is my cowboy's last ride

Cowboy remembers the old trails we rode
And he's back in the saddle tonight
This time I'm lettin' the home fires burn out
And I'm leavin' when I blow out his light
Cause I still remember good waterin' holes
And the places that are open and wide
   And I have decided he won't put me down
   A filly should be free for horsin' around
   And I will no longer be hobbled and tied
This is my cowboy's last ride

SLOW RIDER

I ride an old paint
He's on the weary side
And I'm a saddle tramp
About to cross the Great Divide
Where there's grass in the coulees
And water in the draw
And a forty-pound saddle
Won't make us both raw

Slow rider, slow rider
Move on a little more
The sky boss is waitin'
At the big ranch house door

I can't help but miss 'em
The daughters that I had
One went to Denver
The other went bad
My young wife died
In a pool room fight
But I try to keep singin'
From mornin' till night

Whenever I die
Take my saddle from the wall
Strap it on Snuffy,
Lead him out of the stall
Throw me on his back
And turn toward the West
He knows how to take me
To the spot I love best

NAVAJO

I have seen your colors woven in your blankets
I have heard your names on rivers and on towns
I have seen your turquoise on fine fancy ladies
And the Indian sun is rising instead of goin' down

Navajo, Navajo
The people call the people
From ten thousand years ago
Navajo, Navajo
From the land of the enchantment
    Navajo

I have seen your red rock canyons out of Gallup
I have walked upon your Arizona hills
At Crown Point I watched an artist painting
All the secrets of your past survivin' still

I have seen your women dressed in royal purple
Silver from your hills upon their hands
I don't need a signpost reading 'Reservation'
To know the minute that I'm on Indian land

RAILROADS AND TRAINS

THE LEGEND OF JOHN HENRY'S HAMMER
(with June Carter)

John Henry's pappy woke him up one midnight
He said, 'Before the sheriff comes I want to tell you'
   'Listen, boy,' he said.
  'Learn to ball a jack
  Learn to lay a track
  Learn to pick and shovel too,
    And take my hammer
It'll do anything you tell it to.'

John Henry's mammy had about a dozen babies
John Henry's pappy broke jail about a dozen times
   The babies all got sick
   And when the doctor wanted money
He said, 'I'll pay you a quarter at a time,
   Startin' t'morrow
That's the pay for a steel driver on this line.'

Then the section foreman said:
   'Hey, hammer swinger,
'I see you brought your own hammer, boy
But what else can those muscles do?'

And he said:
   'I can turn a jack
   I can lay a track
   I can pick and shovel, too.'

'Can you swing a hammer, boy?'
'Yes, sir, I do anything you hire me to.'

'Now ain't that somethin'?
So high and mighty with your muscles
Just go ahead, boy, and pick up that hammer,

Pick up the hammer.'
He said, 'Get a rusty spike and swing it down three times
I'll pay you a nickel a day
For every inch you sink it to.
Go on and do what you say you can do.'

With a steep-nosed hammer on a four-foot switch handle
John Henry raised it back till it touched his heels
   The spike went through the cross tie
   And it split it half in two
   Thirty-five cents a day from drivin' steel

Sweat, boy, sweat, sweat
You owe me two more swings

'I was born for drivin' steel.'

Well, John Henry hammered in the mountains
   He give a grunt,
   He give a groan
   With every swing

The women folks for miles around
Heard him and come down
To watch him make the cold steel ring
   Lawd, what a swinger
Just listen to that cold steel ring

But the bad boss come up laughin' at John Henry
Said, 'You full of vinegar now, but you 'bout through.
We gonna get a steam drill to do your share of drivin'
Then what's all the muscles gonna do?
   Huh, John Henry?
Gonna take a little bit of vinegar out of you.'

John Henry said, 'I feed four little brothers

And my baby sister's walkin' on her knees.
   Did the Lord say that machines
   Oughta take the place of livin'?
   And what's a substitute for bread and beans,
     I ain't seen it.
Do engines get rewarded for their steam?'

John Henry hid in a coal mine for his dinner nap
Had thirty minutes to rest before the bell
The mine boss hollered:
   'Get up whoever you are and get a pick axe
   Give me enough coal to start another hell
     and keep it burnin'
   Mind me enough to start another hell.'

John Henry said to his captain:
   'A man ain't nothin' but a man
   But if you'll bring that steam drill 'round
   I'll beat it fair and honest
I'll die with my hammer in my hand
   But I'll be laughin'
Cause you can't replace a steel-drivin' man.'

There was a big crown of people at the mountain
John Henry said to the steam drill,
   'How is you?
Pardon me, Mr Steam Drill,
I s'pose you didn't hear me.
   I said, how is you? Huh?

'Can you turn a jack?
Can you lay a track?
Can you pick and shovel too?
   Listen,
This hammer swinger's talkin' to you.'

RAILROADS AND TRAINS

Two thousand people hollered, 'Go, John Henry!'
Then somebody hollered, 'The mountain's cavin' in'
John Henry told the Cap'n:
 'Tell the kind folks don't to worry
It ain't nothin' but my hammer suckin' wind
 It keeps me breathin'
This steel driver's muscle I ain't tend

'Cap'n, tell the people move back fu'ther
I'm at the finish line and there ain't no drill
It's so far behind but it ain't got the brains to quit it
When she blows up she'll scatter 'cross the hills,
 Lawd, Lawd!
When she blows up she'll scatter 'cross the hills.'

Well, John Henry had a little woman
I believe the lady's name was Polly Ann
 Yea, that was his good woman

John Henry threw his hammer over his shoulder
 And went on home
He laid down to rest his weary back
And early next morning he said:
 'Come here, Polly Ann,
 Come here, sugar.
You know, I believe this is the first time
I ever watched the sun come up
 That I couldn't come up.

'Take my hammer, Polly Ann, and go to that railroad
Swing the hammer like you seen me do it
And when you're swingin' with the lead man
 They'll all know
 They'll all know you're John Henry's woman
But tell 'em, tell 'em that ain't all you can do
Tell 'em

"I can hoist a jack
and I can lay a track
I can pick and shovel too.
  Ain't no machine can
That's been proved to you."

There was a big crowd of mourners at the church house
The section hands laid him in the sand
Trains go by on the rails John Henry laid
They slow down, they take off their hats,
  the men do
When they come to the place where John Henry's layin'
  restin', his back,
Some of 'em say,
  'Mornin' steel driver.
  You sho' was a hammer swinger.'
Then they go on by pickin' up a little speed
  Clickety-clack, clickety-clack
  Clickety-clack, clickety-clack

Yonder lies a steel-drivin' man,
  Lawd, Lawd!
Yonder lies a steel-drivin' man

RAILROADS AND TRAINS

COME AND RIDE THIS TRAIN
(medley)

Come along and ride this train
Come along and ride this train
Cross the mountains,
   prairies,
   reservations,
   rivers,
   levies,
   plains
Come along and ride this train

Ride this train
Ride this train with me to the Mississippi River delta land
A wide stretch of rich black earth
The spreads out along the banks of the Mississippi River
Startin' somewhere up around southern Illinois
And running right on down to the Gulf of Mexico
This is the land of king cotton
This black rich land
And to the people who live here, cotton is their bread and butter
And though the land is rich, to many life is pretty hard

You see that ole shack over there?
That's the home of a sharecropper
   His work is back breakin'
He could spend thirty years of his life into that kind of land
And wind up with that kind of a place
Only to just up and leave with just the clothes on his back
   A prayer in his heart
And a pickup truck half full of used furniture

Ride this train
Ride this train with me
To where the great interstate highways cross the country

146

A hundred years ago over that very ground
    Long before the roads were there
The lonely pony express rider carried the mail
Then came the stagecoach with people and supplies
    Movin' cross country
Today, carryin' on that tradition is the modern mover of America
The man behind the wheel, the truck driver

LOCOMOTIVE MAN

I got a gal in Dallas
I wave at when I go through
I got a gal in Tulsa
That I toot my whistle to
    Tell 'How do'

I got 'em all over the land
I'm a locomotive man

Left my heart in Omaha, Omaha
And I never did quite get it back
I got a Sue in Sioux City
Waitin' by the railroad track
Keeps her money in a tater sack

I got 'em all over the land
I'm a locomotive man

Well, I left a little switch engine
'Bout forty miles south of Bangor, Maine
Couldn't keep a-wheels a-turning
Shouldn't try to pull my train

I got 'em all over the land
I'm a locomotive man

Well, I had a gal in Jackson
And it sure broke my heart to turn her loose
When I checked my time and moved on
She's hooked on my caboose

I got 'em all over the land
I'm a locomotive man

RIDIN' ON THE COTTON BELT

Ridin' on the cotton belt
Cleveland County's where I long to be
I got on at Brinkley
And every mile I make is a memory
This boxcar's cold and windy
And the dust goes around in circles in the air
But my hard times are behind me
And I'm returnin' home
　　So I don't care

And I'm ridin' on the Cotton Belt railroad line
In the pitchin' rollin' rhythm and the noise
Railroad men are friends of mine
And I'm ridin' on the cotton belt, boys

Ridin' on the Cotton Belt
Across the little river called Celine
That's where I went fishin'
And I hunted in her bottoms as a teen
Now just ahead's a farmhouse
And in the kitchen window there's a light
And I just got fourteen dollars
But I'm takin' it and myself home tonight

Jumpin' off the Cotton Belt ain't easy
When she's goin' forty per
But I see my wife standin' there
Hopin' that I'm comin' home to her
I got a few new cuts and bruises
But this ole workin' hobo's made it home
So long to you, Cotton Belt
Thank you for the ride, keep rollin' on

HEY, PORTER

Hey, Porter!
Hey, Porter!
Would you tell me the time?
How much longer will it be
    Till we cross that Mason–Dixon line?
At daylight will you tell that engineer to slow it down
Or better still, just stop the train
    Cause I want to look around

Hey, Porter!
Hey, Porter!
What time, did you say?
How much longer will it be
    Till I can see the light of day?
When we hit Dixie will you tell that engineer
    To ring his bell
And ask everybody that ain't asleep
    To stand right up and yell

Hey, Porter!
Hey, Porter!
It's getting light outside
This old train is puffing smoke
    And I have to strain my eyes
But ask that engineer if he will blow his whistle, please
Cause I smell frost on cotton leaves,
    And I smell that Southern breeze

Hey, Porter!
Hey, Porter!
Please get my bags for me
I need nobody to tell me now that we're in Tennessee
Go tell that engineer
    To make that lonesome whistle scream

We're not far from home
    So take it easy on the steam

Hey, Porter!
Hey, Porter!
Please open up my door
When they stop this train I'm gonna get off first
    Cause I can't wait no more
Tell that engineer I said,
    'Thanks a lot. I didn't mind the fare
I'm gonna set my feet on Southern soil
    And breathe that Southern air.'

SOUTHWIND

Southwind, you picked her up in Jacksonville
And left me cold and lonesome in the rain.
Southwind, you took her off to Nashville,
Left me chokin' in the smoke behind the train.
 And you go Wooo-ooo-oo
She's gone again on the Southwind.

Southwind, I need a forty-dollar ticket
And about this time tomorrow I'll be gone
Southwind, but if I had forty dollars
I would buy myself a smile to carry on
 And you go Wooo-ooo-oo

She's gone again on the Southwind
Southwind, take her fast and take her far
Cause that's the way she always likes to go

Southwind, I will be waitin' for the round-trip
If you bring her back, and I done told her so.
 Don't you go Wooo-ooo-oo
She's gone again on the Southwind

DAUGHTER OF A RAILROAD MAN

Leavin' in a cloud of burning cinders
Cinders from a fire of love gone out
Never lookin' back when she's high-ballin'
She's the daughter of a railroad man no doubt

Wakin' in a new bed every mornin'
Rakin' in a new heart every night
Up and running while the world is sleeping
She's the daughter of a railroad man alright

She is long and sleek and made for movin'
She's outward bound and any time she can
She won't be stayin' long in any station
She's the daughter of a railroad man

Rise out in the night when she gets lonely
You can bet she won't be lonely long
On down the line someone waits her arrival
And the daughter of a railroad man is gone

TRAIN OF LOVE

Train of love's a-comin'
Big black wheels a-hummin'
People waitin' at the station
Happy hearts are drummin'
Train man, tell me maybe
Ain't you got my baby
Ever so often everybody's baby
Gets the urge to roam
But everybody's baby but mine's
    Comin' home

Now stop your whistle blowin'
Cause I've got ways of knowin'
You're bringin' other people's lovers
    But my own keeps goin'
Train of love deceivin'
When she's not gone she's leavin'
Ever so often everybody's baby
Gets the urge to roam
But everybody's baby but mine's
    Comin' home

Train of love now hasten
Sweethearts standin' waitin'
Here and there and everywhere
There's gonna be embracin'
Train man, tell me maybe
Ain't you got my baby
Ever so often everybody's baby
Gets the urge to roam
But everybody's baby but mine's
    Comin' home

Train of love's a-leavin'
Leavin' my heart grievin'
But, early or late, I sit and wait
Because I'm still believin'
We'll walk away together
Though I may wait forever
Ever so often everybody's baby
Gets the urge to roam
But everybody's baby but mine's
  Comin' home

LET THE TRAIN WHISTLE BLOW

I don't want no aggravation
When my train has left the station
If you're there or not, I may not even know
Have a round and remember things
We did that weren't so tender
Let the train blow the whistle when I go

On my old guitar sell tickets
So someone can finally pick it
And tell the girls down at the Ritz I said hello
Tell the gossipers and liars
I will see them in the fire
Let the train blow the whistle when I go

Let her blow
Let her blow
Long and loud
And hard and happy
Let her blow
No regrets
All my debts
Will be paid
When I get laid
Let her blow
Let her blow
Let her blow

You'll be left without excuses
For the evils and abuses
Down to today from years and years ago
And have yourself another toke
From my basket full of smoke
And let the train blow the whistle when I go

PRISONS AND PRISONERS

THE WALLS OF A PRISON

SPOKEN:

It's not always the land that's the hardest and the bitterest
It's the man who has the hard, bitter attitude toward his fellow man.
Or towards the land.
Such is the case that you'll find in this following song, about a man's
    attitude toward his fellow man, and toward his land.

I walked in the big yard to feel the warm sunshine,
A ninety-nine-year man stepped over to me.
He offered a smoke, and he said as I rolled it,
'Tomorrow I'm goin' to break out and go free.

'They watch us by sunlight, they watch us by spotlight.
But I know a way for a man to go free.
Down under my cell I'm diggin' a tunnel,
The walls of a prison will never hold me.'

I told him that I'd have no part of his scheming;
My time would be over one year from today
His eyes blazed with fire, and he looked right through me.
Bitter but broken, again he did say:

'They watch us by sunlight, they watch us by spotlight.
But I know a way for a man to go free.
Down under my cell I'm diggin' a tunnel,
The walls of a prison will never hold me.'

Next mornin' at breakfast, the old man was missing;
Then we all heard the rifles high up on the wall
He'd gone through the tunnel, just like he had promised,
And they said he was cryin' when they saw him fall.

PRISONS AND PRISONERS

FOLSOM PRISON BLUES

I hear the train a-comin'
It's rollin' round the bend
And I ain't seen the sunshine
Since I don't know when
I'm stuck in Folsom Prison
And time keeps draggin' on
But that train keeps a-rollin'
On down to San Antone

When I was just a baby
My mama told me, 'Son,
Always be a good boy;
Don't ever play with guns.'
But I shot a man in Reno
Just to watch him die.
When I hear that whistle blowin'
I hang my head and cry.

I bet there's rich folks eatin'
In a fancy dining car.
They're prob'ly drinkin' coffee
And smokin' big cigars,
But I know I had it comin',
I know I can't be free.
But those people keep a-movin',
And that's what tortures me.

Well, if they freed me from this prison,
If that railroad train was mine,
I bet I'd move it on
A little farther down the line.
Far from Folsom Prison,
That's where I want to stay,
And I'd let that lonesome whistle
    Blow my blues away

JOHNNY CASH THE SONGS

SEND A PICTURE OF MOTHER

After seven years behind these bars together
I'll miss you more than a brother when you go
   When you go
If only I had not tried to escape
They'd pardon me with you, I know
   Yes, I know
Won't you tell the folks back home
I'll soon be comin'
And don't let 'em know I never will be free
   Be free
Sometimes write and tell me how they're doin'
And send a picture of mother back to me

Say hello to Dad and shake his poor hard-workin' hand
And send a picture of mother if you can

I'm happy for you that you got your freedom
But stay with me just another minute or so
   Or so
After all this sweat and blood together
Who'll be my fightin' partner when you go
   When you go?

The hardest time will be on Sunday mornin'
Church bells will ring on heaven hill
Heaven hill
Please ask Reverend Garrett to pray for me
And send a picture of mother if you will

Say hello to Dad and shake his poor hard-workin' hand
And send a picture of mother if you can

DEAR MRS
(with Andrew J. Arnette Jr)

Dear Mrs though we have never met
I know very much about you
I know that you've got hair that shines
   Like the morning sun
You've got eyes that hold the blueness of the sky
And of the deepest sea on a clear day
And a smile that has the sparkle of a diamond

I know that because I've heard him say
   Those things about you
These are the thoughts and the words of a man
Who spent many heartbreaking years behind prison walls
The father of your children
The man who worshipped the very ground that you walk on

He had a picture of you, Mrs
It was old and faded and torn
But you could tell at a glance
That he never exaggerated in his thoughts and visions

He never left his cell without first checking
To see if he had your picture with him

He was a young man when he first came to prison
And he talked a great deal about you
But as the years passed he talked less and less
And during his last year here
I don't believe he ever said a word to anybody

He had the appearance of a man
Much older than he really was
He walked with his head down and his shoulders sagging
And the walk itself seemed to take a great deal of effort

He never received a letter or had a visitor
   While he was here in prison
But never did he stop looking and waiting
Every day at mail call you could see him standing
   Close to his bars
With the look of a child awaiting a reward
Even after the mailman had passed his cell
His pleading eyes would follow
   Begging

As always he'd feel of his shirt pocket
And then just stand there staring at the emptiness
And, as always, I could somehow feel
The lump in his throat and the burning of his eyes
You know, Mrs, like just before you start to cry

Well, I thought you might like to know
That they buried his body today
   Just outside the prison walls
They buried him there because nobody cared enough
   To claim his body
You know there was even a couple of old convicts there
   That actually cried
No, not because they cared for him
But for what he died from, they cared for
   Loneliness

Every prisoner knows loneliness
But some know it more than others
The man they buried today had died many times
Every day he waited, hoping and praying
   For a letter or card
Or just a note or anything to let him know that
Somewhere out there somebody cared for him
   That assurance never came
And today, he died, Mrs

PRISONS AND PRISONERS

He died from loneliness,
    Starved for love
A love that nobody wanted

You see, no man, woman or child is immune
To the need of love
    Or to be loved
No matter how terrible his crime might have been

The death he died from today was more inhuman
    But his suffering is over now
And he's resting in a pauper's grave in a prison suit
And in his pocket is an old torn and faded picture
    Of, yes, of you, Mrs

AUSTIN PRISON

They had a warrant out for me all over the country
And I was tryin' to beat the raps in Idaho
I was breakin' into a schoolhouse Sunday mornin'
   Without warnin',
When I saw a sheriff comin' for me slow down from below

His steel grey eyes were blazin' when he saw me
His hand was on his gun when he rode up
He said: 'You killed that woman, I know you shot her,
   Why'd you do it?
I'm takin' you to Austin, then I'm gonna lock you up.'

Well, he tied me with a blow iron the next mornin'
And he had me deep in Texas the next day
A crazy, screamin' lynch mob waited
   In the streets of Austin
But he put me in the jailhouse, and he threw away the key

A jury found me guilty three months later,
Twelve men with murder in their eyes
They even took me out and said,
   'Now, show us where you killed her!'
And the wicked judge said,
   'Now I hereby sentence you to die.'

But here I am quite a way from Austin Prison;
My friend, the jailer, handed me a file
Now all I want between me and there
   Are a lot of friendly people
And miles and miles
   And miles and miles
   And miles and miles
   And miles

CITY JAIL

City Jail, City Jail
Like an old scared dog I tuck my tail
Hang my head and not a careless word is said
I gotta sleep on the floor once more
    At the city jail

Well, I was hangin' around the bus station
Mindin' my own business like I always do
When I saw this waitress in this bus station cafe
And I thought I'd check out the action
    Like I always do
I give her the bad eye
And made a few choice personal comments
About what I thought mine and her possibilities
    Could be for a team
When she called the badge on me
The badge grabbed me by the arm and said,
    'What are you doing hanging around here for?'
And I said, 'For whatever's goin' around.'

He said, 'No, what I mean is, what are you doing saying
    Things like that to that lady?'
And I said, 'What's that lady doing with purple hair?'
Well, the badge man said, 'You a smart aleck'
And I said, 'No, I ain't. I'm just hungry.'
And he said, 'You're acting like a smart aleck'
I said, 'No, it's how I act when I get hungry.'

Well, he put me outside in a dark corner
And before you could say hypocrite he hit me on the head
And I said, 'Ohhhhhh, don't hit me on the head
    I can't protect myself with the handcuffs on
    Please don't hit me on the head.'

And he hit me again,
And he hit me again,
And he hit me again
And I said,
    'Oh, oh, oh, oh,
    Please don't stand on my feet when you hit me
    I'll break my ankles when I fall.'

Well, about that time he threw me in the wagon
And that waitress walked out with a sailor
    I said, 'Hey you. Not you,
    I'm talkin' to the purple people-eater
    Yes, you, lady,
    Quote you're the cause of it all unquote.'

Then she said to the sailor, said,
'Get me away from that horrible man, Harry.'

Well, as they hauled me away I said,
    'Everybody have a nice evening.'

PRISONS AND PRISONERS

SAN QUENTIN

San Quentin, you've been livin' hell to me
You've hosted me since nineteen sixty-three
I've seen 'em come and go, and I've seen 'em die
And long ago I stopped askin' why

San Quentin, I hate every inch of you
You've cut me and have scarred me through and through
And I'll walk out a wiser, weaker man
Mister Congressman, you can't understand

San Quentin, what good do you think you do?
Do you think I'll be different when you're through?
You bent my heart and mind and you warped my soul
And your stone walls turn my blood a little cold

San Quentin, may you rot and burn in hell.
May your walls fall and may I live to tell
May all the world forget you ever stood
And may all the world regret you did no good

San Quentin, I hate every inch of you

THIS SIDE OF THE LAW

On this side of the law,
On that side of the law
   Who is right?
   Who is wrong?
   Who is weak?
   Who is strong?
Who is for and who's against the law?

You see, I didn't really mean any harm
But I simply couldn't make it on the farm
When the land won't give a lot
You gotta do with what you got
And all I got's the muscle in my arm
   'Bum! bum! bum!'

Well, I wouldn't ever hurt my fellow man
And it seems to me that you could understand
I'm just tryin' to help myself without hurtin' somebody else
And a man has go to do the best he can

Well, I didn't mean to let my family down
And I'm not giving you the runaround
I'd much rather be dead than have to beg my daily bread
And to pay my way no matter where I'm bound
   'Bum! bum! bum!'

Well, I didn't really think that I did wrong
So long as I stayed here where I belong
I did the only thing I could same as anybody would
And I was simply trying to get along

MICHIGAN CITY HOWDY DO

Well, Johnson Van Dyke Grigsby
Was paroled at eighty-nine
He'd never walked on a carpet
Never tasted dinner wine
His ole eyes were slowly fadin'
As he walked out of the gate
And he breathed the first free air he'd breathed
    Since 1908

Howdy do, Michigan City
You're sure a pretty sight
But I know there's bigger cities
And more exciting lives
But I think your girls are pretty
And I love your children too
Michigan City, Indiana, howdy do
Michigan City, Indiana, howdy do

Filled with the joy of freedom
He didn't know that he was old
Cause time don't really matter
When it's bubblin' in your soul
Well, I don't think he was bitter
Cause he sure had a smile
And down the streets of Michigan City
He walked his first free mile

JACOB GREEN

Jacob Green got busted for possession
Next morning early he appeared in court
But he was sent to jail to wait
To be tried at some later date
Next morning early there came a sad report
At the jail they took away his clothes to shame him
And to make sure Jacob Green had no pride left
They cut off all his hair
Today they found him hanging there
Afraid to face the day,
   He killed himself

It happened yesterday
And if you turn your head away
Somewhere in some dirty hole
The scene will be rerun
Not only Jacob Green
But many more you've never seen
It could be someone that you love gets done
   Like Jacob Green got done
It could be someone that you love gets done
   Like Jacob Green got done

Jacob's father hired a team of lawyers
Inspections and long inquiries were held
The sheriff then retired
And the paper said two guards were fired
They put a brand-new coat of paint on Jacob's cell
But like a tomb that looks so white and shiny
Inside, you'll find corruption never seen
And somewhere out there tonight
In a dirty cell without a light
They'll be locking up another Jacob Green

SOLDIERS AND WARS

ROUTE #1, BOX 144

His dying barely made the morning paper;
And they summed it up in twenty words or more

'Killed in action, leaves wife and baby, at Route One, Box One Forty-
   four'

He grew up on a little farm just a couple of miles out of town. As a
   boy, he worked in his daddy's field. And, when his daddy could
   spare him, he hired out to the neighbors for whatever they could
   pay him. He was thought of as just average: a good boy, nothin'
   more, the average amount of friends

He married his high school sweetheart. They bought a little plot of
   ground. A couple of miles out of town on the mailbox, it said,
   'Route #1, Box 144'; hardly ever came to town – except for
   maybe on Saturdays. Of course, the usual crew was always there,
   but he didn't spend a lot of time with the usual crew. He took care
   of his business: bought what he had to have or could afford for
   his family, and went back to his little farm

With a baby on the way, he went to the army. And it was just a short
   while that the news came that he was killed in action. His body
   was sent back on a plane, and then by train. And then, they
   brought the body from the train station to Route 1, Box 144

He never did great things to be remembered;
He had never been away from home before
But you'd've thought he was president or something
   At Route One, Box One Forty-four.

A CROFT IN CLACHAN
(The Ballad of Rob MacDunn)

With the Campbells and the MacDonalds,
It was in their blood to fight
With each passing generation
It became a man's birthright
But they always had one common enemy
Never would the English crown
Take Scottish independency

Oh, the battles raged in Glasgow
    And majestic Edinburgh
    And they came with war machines
    And in the Highlands shots were heard
    Then the people rose in union
    And the forces moved as one
    And the clans all joined together
    To see English on the run

And in a tiny croft in Clachan set a mother,
    Peg MacDunn
And she sewed a coat together
For her sixteen-year son
And she cried as he was leaving
    'Don't forget to keep ye warm
    And come ye back to Clachan
    When the English are all done'

Now Rob MacDunn was ready
As he left the croft behind
And he joined the Highland pipe brigade
With one thing on his mind
That to keep his home and freedom
He must face it like a man
So he marched in common cadence
With his musket in his hand

And he met the hills of battle
In the Highlands and the Low
And the reason for the fighting
Long was in his blood to know
In the idle of the rumble
He went forward gaining ground
And the bagpipes still were pipin'
As the dead lay all around

Then he moved with no direction
Till he faced the winds of north
And he boldly climbed a Highlands
Farther from the Firth of Forth

Then one freezing blowing morning
Came the cry of Peg MacDunn
'Back to my croft in Clachan
God has sent me home my son.'

And in another croft in Clachan
Cross the way from the MacDunns
With her face against the window
Stood a young girl tired and worn
And she smiled a secret knowing
As she breathed a prayer alone
'I thank thee, Lord, for bringing
Rob MacDunn back safely home.'

Back to the croft in Clachan
He returned to peace again
He had gone abroad at sixteen
But he came back as a man

THE BIG BATTLE

I think, sir, the battle is over
And the young soldier laid down his gun
I'm tired of running for cover
I'm certain the battle is done

Oh, see over there where we fought them
It's quiet for they've all gone away
All that's left is the dead and the dying
The Blue lying 'long side the Gray

So you think the battle is over,
And you even lay down your gun
You carelessly rise from your cover
For you think the battle is done

Now, boy, hit the dirt;
    Listen to me,
For I'm still the one in command
Get flat on the ground here beside me
And lay your ear hard to the sand

Can you hear the deafening rumble?
Can you feel the trembling ground?
It's not just the horses and wagons
That make such a deafening sound

For ev'ry shot fired has an echo
And ev'ry man killed wanted life
There lies your friend Jim McKenney
Can you take the news to his wife?

No, son, the battle's not over
You'll see that it's only begun
The rest of the battle will cover
The part that has blackened the sun

JOHNNY CASH THE SONGS

The fight yet to come's not with cannon,
Nor will the fight be hand to hand
   No one will regroup the forces;
No charge will a general command

The battle will rage in the bosom
Of mother and sweetheart and wife
   Brother and sister and daughter
Will grieve for the rest of their lives

Now, go ahead, rise from your cover
Be thankful that God let you live
Go fight the rest of the battle
For those who gave all they could give

I see, sir, the battle's not over
The battle has only begun
The rest of the battle will cover
This part that has blackened the sun

For tho' there's no sound of the cannon
And tho' there's no smoke in the sky
I'm dropping the gun and the saber
And ready for battle am I

LIKE A SOLDIER

With the twilight colors falling
And the evening layin' shadows
Hidden memories come stealin' from my mind
And I feel my own heart beatin' out
The simple joy of livin'
And I wonder how I ever was that kind

But the wild road I was ramblin'
Was always out there callin'
And you said a hundred times I should've died
Then you reached down and touched me
And lifted me up with you
So I believe it was a road I was meant to ride

I'm like a soldier gettin' over the war
I'm like a young man gettin' over his crazy days
Like a bandit gettin' over his lawless ways
I don't have to do that anymore
I'm like a soldier gettin' over the war

There are nights I don't remember
And pain that's been forgotten
And a lot of things I choose not to recall
There are faces that come to me
In my darkest secret memories
Faces that I wish would not come back at all

But in my dream's parade of lovers
From the other times and places
There's not one that matters now, no matter who
I'm just thankful for the journey
And that I survived the battles
And that my spoils of victory is you

I'm like a soldier gettin' over the war
I'm like a young man gettin' over his crazy days
Like a bandit gettin' over his lawless ways
Every day gets better than the day before
I'm like a soldier gettin' over the war

SOLDIERS AND WARS

PATRIOT

THESE ARE MY PEOPLE

These are my people
This is the land where my forefathers lie
These are my people
In brotherhood we're heirs of a creed to live by
A creed that proclaims
That by loved ones' blood stains
This is my land
And these are my people

These are my people
They were born on and lived by the land
These are my people
And their cities were raised by hardworking hands
And their faces do tell
That they're holding on well
To this, their land
Yes, these are my people

These are my people
These are the ones who will reach for the stars
These are my people
That are the light of the earth
You can tell they are ours
A new step to take
And a new day will break
For this, my land
Yes, these are my people

These are my people
ummm, ummm, ummm

SOLD OUT OF FLAGPOLES

I walked down past the courthouse square
Three blocks or maybe four
Run into my old friend there
That runs a handy hardware store
I said, 'Mornin', Loney, what's the good word?'
He said, 'Abraham Lincoln, the Lone Ranger, Mickey Mouse
    And I'm sold out of flagpoles'

I popped the top of a soda pop
Laid a quarter on the bar
I said, 'Inflation is a dirty dog
And payday sure ain't goin' far.'
'Liberty,' said Loney
'E pluribus unum
In God we trust
    And I'm sold out of flagpoles'

And I said, 'Hey, Loney, did you see Evil Knievel
    jumping on TV?
Jumped thirteen buses with his mo-sheen
Reckon he could jump fourteen?'

'No doubt,' said Loney
'Winners keep on winning
And even losers win sometimes
    And I'm sold out of flagpoles'

'Ain't this been a year,' I said
'With frost and blight and flood and drought
Twice as many tornadoes
Reckon it's all caused by fallout.'
'Nah, it's the seasons,' said Loney
    'They change;
The wind's gonna blow, always did
    And I'm sold out of flagpoles'

JOHNNY CASH THE SONGS

'Hey, watcha think about the sheriff's daughter
Running off with the preacher's son?
The sheriff's wife had to hold him back
From goin' after them with his gun'

'Boys and girls,' said Loney
'Will get together;
Everything's normal
    And I'm sold out of flagpoles'

RAGGED OLD FLAG

I walked through a country courthouse square,
On a park bench an old man was sitting there.
I said, 'Your old courthouse is kinda run down.'
He said, 'Naw, it'll do for our little town.'
I said, 'Your flagpole has leaned a little bit,
And that ragged old flag you got hanging on it.'

He said, 'Have a seat,' and I sat down.
'Is this the first time you've been to our little town?'
I said, 'I think it is.' He said, 'I don't like to brag,
But we're kinda proud of that ragged old flag.

'You see, we got a little hole in that flag there
When Washington took it across the Delaware.
And it got powder-burned the night Francis Scott Key
Sat watching it writing "Say can you see".
And it got a bad rip in New Orleans
With Packingham and Jackson tuggin' at its seams.

'And it almost fell at the Alamo
Beside the Texas flag, but she waved on through.
She got cut with a sword at Chancellorsville
And she got cut again at Shiloh Hill.
There was Robert E. Lee, Beauregard and Bragg,
And the South wind blew hard on that ragged old flag.

'On Flanders Field in World War I
She got a big hole from a Bertha gun.
She turned blood-red in World War II
She hung limp and low by the time it was through.
She was in Korea and Vietnam
She went where she was sent by her Uncle Sam.
She waved from our ships upon the briny foam,
And now they're about quit waving her back here at home.

In her own good land here she's been abused –
She's been burned, dishonoured, denied and refused.

'And the government for which she stands
Is scandalized throughout the land.
And she's getting threadbare and wearing thin,
But she's in good shape for the shape she's in.
Cause she's been through the fire before
And I believe she can take a whole lot more.

'So we raise her up every morning,
    Take her down every night.
We don't let her touch the ground and we hold her up right.
On second thought, I do like to brag,
Cause I'm mighty proud of that Ragged Old Flag.'

SINGIN' IN VIET NAM TALKIN' BLUES

One mornin' at breakfast I said to my wife,
'We been everywhere once and some places twice'
As I had another helpin' of country ham
She said, 'We ain't never been to Viet Nam
And there's a bunch of our boys over there'
   So we went
   To the Orient,
      Saigon

Well, we got a big welcome when we drove in
Through the gates of a place that they call Long Binh
We checked in and everything got kinda quiet
But a soldier boy said, 'Just wait till tonight
   Things get noisy
   Things start happenin'
   Big, bad firecrackers'

Well, that night we did about four shows for the boys
And they were livin' it up with a whole lot of noise
We did our last song for the night
And we crawled into bed for some peace and quiet
   But things weren't peaceful
   And things weren't quiet
   Things were scary

Well, for a few minutes June never said one word
And I thought at first she hadn't heard
Then a shell exploded not two miles away
She sat up in bed and I heard her say
   'What was that?'
   I said, 'That was a shell, or a bomb.'
   She said, 'I'm scared.'
   I said, 'Me too.'

Well, all night long that noise kept on
And the sound would chill you right to the bone
The bullets and the bombs and the mortar shells
Shook our bed every time one fell
   And it never let up
   It was going to get worse
   Before it got any better

Well, when the sun came up, the noise died down
We got a few minutes' sleep and we was sleepin' sound
Then a soldier knocked on our door and said
Last night they brought in seven dead and fourteen wounded
And would we come down to the base hospital and see the boys
   'Yeah.'

So we went to the hospital ward by day
And every night we was singin' away
Then the shells and the bombs took on again
And the helicopters brought in the wounded men
   Night after night,
   Day after day,
   Comin' and a-goin'

So we sadly sang for them our last song
And reluctantly we said so long
We did our best to let 'em know that we care
For every last one of them that's over there
   Whether we belong over there or not
   Somebody over here loves 'em and needs 'em

Well, now that's about all that there is to tell
About that little trip and the livin' hell
And if I ever go back over there any more
I hope there's none of our boys there for me to sing for
   I hope that war over there is over with
   And they all come back home
   To stay
   In peace

DRIVE ON

Well, I got a friend named Whiskey Sam
He was my boonie rat buddy for a year in Nam
He said, I think my country got a little off track,
Took 'em twenty-five years to welcome me back

But it's better than not coming back at all
Many a good man I saw fall
And even now every time I dream
I hear the men and the monkeys in the jungle scream

Drive on
It don't mean nothin'
My children love me
But they don't understand
And I got a woman who knows her man
Drive on
It don't mean nothin'
It don't mean nothin'
Drive on

Well, I remember one night Tex and me
Rappelled in on a hot L-Z
We had our 16's on rock'n'roll
And with all that fire
I was scared and cold

I was crazy and I was wild
And I have seen the tiger smile
I spit in a bamboo viper's face
And I'd be dead but by God's grace

It was a slow walk in a sad rain
And nobody tried to be John Wayne
I came home but Tex did not
And I can't talk about the hit he got

But I got a little limp now when I walk
And I got a little tremelo when I talk
But my letter read from Whiskey Sam:
You're a walkin' talkin' miracle from Viet Nam

Drive on

PEOPLE

GIVE MY LOVE TO ROSE

I found him by the railroad track this mornin'
I could see that he was nearly dead
I knelt down beside him and I listened
Just to hear the words the dyin' fellow said

He said, 'They let me out of prison out in 'Frisco
For ten long years I paid for what I'd done
I was tryin' to get back to Louisiana
To see my Rose and get to know my son

'Give my love to Rose, please, won't you, Mister?
Take her all my money, tell her buy some pretty clothes
Tell the boy that Daddy's so proud of him
And don't forget to give my love to Rose

'Wontcha tell them I said thanks for waiting for me?
Tell my boy to help his mom at home
Tell my Rose to try to find another
Cause it ain't right that she should live alone

'Mister, here's the bag with all the money
It won't last them long the way it goes
God bless you for findin' me this mornin'
Now don't forget to give my love to Rose.'

MY OLD FADED ROSE
(with June Carter)

Oh, you have got 'em all hangin' around
Like the fringes on your gown
You're pickin' 'em up and a-layin' 'em low
   My old faded rose

Was it me that said you're a-gettin' old
And a-losin' your appeal?
Was it me that said you're growin' cold
And I wanted another deal?
Well, I see that you're not wilted
And you sure fill out your clothes
Why didn't I know about the fiery glow
   In my old faded rose?

My old faded rose
With your petals hangin' down
I didn't know I'd miss you so
   My old faded rose
Ah, look at 'em a-hangin' around
Like the fringes on your gown
You're pickin' 'em up and a-layin' 'em low
   My old faded rose

Well, now I didn't mean
That other grass was green
And your leaves are turnin' brown
Don't take me seriously
When I tell you don't a-hang around
I see you don't need prunin'
Now who do you suppose
Is back in line for one more time
   With my old faded rose?

JOHNNY CASH THE SONGS

CALL DADDY FROM THE MINE

A little girl woke up deep in the dark and started crying
The mother brought a light and held her daughter tight
   She thought it was so strange
   To hear a little girl of nine cry
Call Daddy from the mine
Call Daddy from the mine

The mother wiped the tears and said:
'See, honey, you're only dreaming
Your dad must work today; he has to draw his pay.'
   She left her then but still could hear
   Her cry time after time
Call Daddy from the mine
Call Daddy from the mine

Then the countryside was shaken by a mighty rumble
And feared for miles around was the tremblin' of the ground
   The little girl was fast asleep
   Yet cried out one more time
Call Daddy from the mine
Call Daddy from the mine

Ten thousand tears and two weeks later
Deep in the smoking ground
A dyin' man was found, had survived all those around
He'd quickly crawled to a fresh pocket of air
   Barely just in time
   When he heard his own child whine
Call Daddy from the mine
Call Daddy from the mine

THE FROZEN FOUR-HUNDRED-POUND
FAIR-TO-MIDDLIN' COTTON PICKER

I left the field one evenin'
My fingers so cold and sore
From fair-to-middlin' cotton
Three hundred pounds or more

Jim McCann was still pickin'
Straddlin' his row
The sun began to sinkin'
And the wind began to blow

He was bound to get four hundred
A-draggin' a twelve-foot sack
I hollered out, 'Jim, come weigh it'
But I only saw his back

So I went on home to supper
And gathered around my kin
I was thinkin' of Jim out there pickin'
With winter settin' in

Next morning the air was freezing
The snow was nine feet deep
I jerked on my long red handles
And I left my kids asleep

I got myself a shovel
And went to where I seen Jim go
And commenced to a-diggin' for him
At the other end of his row

I found his body frozen
And I took him in to thaw
I dug in his sack and I waited
And I added Jim's marks that I saw

JOHNNY CASH THE SONGS

The total was over four hundred
So he picked more than he bet
Of fair-to-middlin' cotton
But Jim ain't thawed out yet

THE MASTERPIECE

RECITATION:

There was an old stone-cutter who lived in a cabin on the mountainside
And the old stone-cutter knew it wouldn't be long before he died
And all around his cabin were statues the man had made
Statues that the buyers said were all of a mediocre grade
With his calloused hands he lit a lamp and laid down his head on his handmade table
And he softly whispered, 'Lord, I'm old and shaky and I'm hardly able
But give me strength and wisdom and give me a week at least
And I'll climb up to the top of this mountain and chisel out a masterpiece.'

The very next morning he felt new strength and he took his brand-new hammer and a sharpest chisel
He began to climb the mountain, his old feet slipping in the freezing drizzle
When he finally reached the top, he shouted to a world that didn't want to hear
'I'll carve my masterpiece out of this marble boulder here.'

So the hammer beat the chisel and he hammered 'til an image grew
Then he stopped to look it over, to appraise his work when he was through
It was a boy carryin' a crippled boy and the old man said, 'It isn't my masterpiece
I'll call it "Charity" and then a masterpiece mine will be.'

So the hammer beat the chisel 'til another image in the marble grew
Then the wind began to blowin' and he set and rested when he was through
It was the image of a mother holding her child; he said, 'This is love as the world would know

But it isn't my masterpiece' and he began again as it began to snow

The hammer bat the chisel as the snow fell harder and the wind
   grew and grew
He feel to his knees holding a stone and he threw down his hammer
   and his chisel too
He lay frozen face down in the snow but one hand was held for the
   world to see
Cut in the marble was his masterpiece
   Three neatly carved letters,
   G-O-D

THE TIMBER MAN

Well, my world is green and dark and damp
My home is in the loggin' camp
All week I cut down the mighty trees
Saturday I get to do as I please

I give the man more than his hire
And he'll never know it if I tire
Show me the toughest tree around
The timber man will bring it down

Swing it hard, cut it clean
No halfway or in between
Move when the axe is in my hand
Make way for the timber man

SPOKEN:
 Yea, he was a mighty big tough man, usually
 That timber man that lived in that forest
 And cut down those big trees

Well, they say there's sawdust in my brain
And don't get caught out in the rain
I got stump water in my blood
The sweat from my brow turns the ground to mud

When the men don't know how to fell a tree
The one they'll come and ask is me
I mark my spot and I'll take my stand
The tree's gonna fall for the timber man

SPOKEN:
 And when they're cuttin' on a tree
 And it's just about ready to fall
 The man yells out
 Tiiimmmmmmmmmmmberrrrrrrrr!!!

YOU AND TENNESSEE

I stayed away too long, I know
And every day was slow to go
Every night I dreamed I was here
It's been a mighty lonely year

Every mile I needed you
I kinda hoped that you needed me too
Everywhere I saw your face
Around every town I was in
This old familiar place welcomed me again
Back to where I belong to be
   Back to you and Tennessee
   Back to you and Tennessee

Beside the Cumberland River
Where the grass is soft and sweet
We ran across the fields of cedar
Hiding from the noisy streets

And when the leaves fell from the cold
The stars were silver, the moon was gold
I said, it's yours with love from me
I'm planting my roots in this ground

And if they look for me I'll be found
With something that is part of me
   You and Tennessee
   Back with you and Tennessee

CISCO CLIFTON'S FILLIN' STATION

RECITATION:

Cisco Clifton had a fillin' station about a mile and a half from town;
Most cars passed, unless they were out of gas, so Cisco was always
    around
Regular gas was all that he sold, except tobacco, matches, and oil
Other than that, he fixed lots of flats, keeping Cisco's rough hands
    soiled.
He'd wipe the glass and check the air and a hundred times a day
He patiently gave directions on how to get to the state highway.

He usually would give 'em water, or a tire or two, some air,
And once a big black Cadillac spent seven dollars there.
He'd give anybody anything they'd ask and lend anything he had;
His tools, or tires, bumper jacks, or wire, the good ones or the bad.

In winter time there was a depot stove and a table for the checker
    game.
And ev'ry mornin' at sun-up the same checker players came.
So Cisco Clifton's fillin' station was always in the red;
Personal loans were personally gone, but never a word was said.

One mornin' at eight, the checker players heard a bulldozer roar like
    a freight,
And Cisco said, 'I hope my kids stay fed, when they build that
    interstate.'
It managed to pay for the property where the little fillin' station sat,
And friends still came for the checker games, so Cisco settled for
    that.

He wouldn't say so, but Cisco knew that the interstate was too much
    to fight,
But to keep his will, and to pay his bills, he did odd jobs at night.
He still opened up at sunrise and the checker game went on;

The cars flew past on high test gas, and the neighbors had sold out and gone.

If a car ever did go by, he was lost, and if he stopped, they were treated the same,
So at Cisco Clifton's fillin' station, there's a 'Howdy' and a checker game.

PEOPLE

THE BALLAD OF BARBARA

In a southern town where I was born
That's where I got my education
　　I worked in the fields
　　And I walked in the woods
And I wondered at Creation

I recall the sun in a sky of blue
And the smell of green things growin'
　　And the seasons changed
　　And I lived each day
Just the way the wind was blowin'

Then I heard of a cultured city life
Breathtaking lofty steeples
And the day I called myself a man
I left my land and my people

And I rambled north
And I rambled east
And I tested and I tasted
And a girl or two
Took me round and round
But they always left me wasted

In a world that's all concrete and steel
With nothing green ever growin'
Where the buildings hide the rising sun
And they block the free wind from blowin'

When you sleep all day
And you wake all night
To a world of drink and laughter
I met that girl that I was sure would be
The one that I was after

In a soft blue gown and a formal tux
Beneath that lofty steeple
He said, 'Do you, Barbara, take this man
Will you be one of his people?'
  And she said, 'I will.'
  And she said, 'I do.'
And the world looked mighty pretty
And we lived in a fancy downtown flat
Cause she loved the noisy city

But the days grew cold beneath the yellow sky
And I longed for green things growin'
And I talked of home and the people there
But she'd not agree to goin'
Then her hazel eyes turned away from me
With a look that wasn't pretty
And she turned into concrete and steel
And she said, 'I'll take the city.'

Now the cars go by on the interstate
And my pack is on my shoulder
But I'm goin' home where I belong
  Much wiser now and older

ABNER BROWN

SPOKEN:

    Every town has its town bum, I guess
      Ours had one
    Here's a song about him
    I remember him fondly well
      His name was Abner Brown

I knew an old drunk
Named Abner Brown
Nobody knew when he came to town
But he spread goodwill to his fellow men
And they let him sleep in the cotton gin
He could drink more brew than an army could
But he had more friends and he did more good
Than a lot of fine fancy people in our town
    So they tolerated Abner Brown

And all us kids were on his side cause he told us tales
Till our eyes grew wide
And he made us feel 'bout ten feet tall
Cause he had no kids but he claimed us all

And after school and on weekends
You could find men down at the cotton gin
The truest friend that I ever found
Was a good ole drunk named Abner Brown

Abner Brown, I wish that I could see you once again
I believe that you'd stack up
With all the mighty men I've met and known
On all the low and higher places I've been
Thinking of you picks me up when I'm feeling down
I thank the Lord for making Abner Brown

210

Lord, take me back to the cotton land
To Arkansas, take me home again
Let me be the boy that I had once been
Let me walk that road to the cotton gin

He's probably dead many years ago
Gone the way that old drunks go
But I still like to sit me down
Talk to my old friend Abner Brown

THE MATADOR
(with June Carter)

The crowd is waiting for the bullfight
   Matador
My final fight
The place is packed once more

But Anita won't throw me a rose this fight
The one she wears is not for me tonight

She's watching now with her new love, I know
   Walk proud and slow
He's strong and sure and gives the crowd their show
   They want blood, you know
You're still their idol
As you were before
Kill just once more
Remind Anita you're the greatest
   Matador

Walk on out, forget Anita in the stands
Be a tall and brave and noble man
Be better than you've ever been before
Make this your greatest moment
   Matador

THE CARETAKER

I live in the cemetery
Old caretaker they call me
In the wintertime I rake the leaves
And in summer I cut the weeds

When a funeral comes the people cry and pray
They bury their dead and they all go away
But through their grief I still can see
Their hate and greed and jealousy

So here I work and I somehow hide
From a world that rushes by our side
And each night when I rest my head
I'm contented as the peaceful dead

But who's gonna cry when ole John dies?
But who's gonna cry when ole John dies?

Once I was a young man
Dashing with the girls
Now no one wants an old man
I lost my handsome curls
But I want to say when my time comes
Lay me facing the rising sun
Put me in a corner where I buried my pup
Tell the preacher to pray then cover me up

Don't lay flowers where my head should be
Maybe God will let some grow for me
And all the little children that I loved like my own
Will they be sorry that ole John's gone?

But who's gonna cry when ole John dies?
Who's gonna cry when ole John dies?

DORRAINE OF PONCHARTRAIN

As I walked by the lake one day
By chance my Dorraine passed my way
Then she and I walked hand in hand
On the banks of Ponchartrain
     I pinned a flower on her heart
     I swore we'd never be apart
She vowed her love forever
And as I kissed her did the same

Dorraine, my Dorraine
My dark-haired little angel
My belle of Ponchartrain

We set down on the dock
And with our hearts and fingers locked
We laughed and talked and joked about
When our names are the same
     And joking I said, 'Honey,
     Are you marryin' me for money?'
And it took just one quick look to tell
It hurt my dear Dorraine

She jumped and stood above me
And she cried, 'Why don't you love me?'
I'm rowin' home across the lake
You won't see me again.'
     I called and called some more
     But she rowed fast from the shore
And the clouds brought by a wind
Began to rain on Ponchartrain

Dorraine, I called Dorraine
Come back, my little angel
My belle of Ponchartrain

The storm should make her learn
That she should make a swift return
But as the rain fell harder
I lost sight of my Dorraine
   As panic gripped my heart
   I drew the oars and made my start
To look for her on ragin' waters
And the rain on Ponchartrain

At darkness I still called
But no one heard my cries at all
And when the daybreak came then
Others helped me look for my Dorraine
   But there was not a thing afloat
   Except the oars from her rowboat
For all was lost upon the choppy waves
And rain on Ponchartrain

Now I come day after day
To where my sweetheart rowed away
And I gaze across the water
Of the reigning Ponchartrain
   Just one thing and nothing more
   Ever floated back to shore
Was the flower I hold
It was the one
I pinned on my Dorraine

Dorraine, my Dorraine
My dark-haired little angel
My belle of Ponchartrain

CALILOU

Well, I'm finally goin' back to Louisiana
Runnin' and thumbin' all the way
Started out way out in California
I been makin' 'bout 500 miles a day
I covered all the beaches on the West Coast
From Mexico to Crescent City Bay
But Calilou was not in California
That's where her daddy came from, by the way
And by the way, her mother was a Cajun
She came from New Orleans I've heard her say
And it's just like a girl to want to see her mama
So I might find her there or on the way

Calilou, Calilou
Well, they should have called you restless
And they should have called you drifter
Yea, they should have called you trouble
    Instead of Calilou

I recall the first time that I saw her
I picked her up near Phoenix in my car
Just another beauty seeking fame and fortune
And I told her she should be a movie star
The next time I saw her was Tucumcari
She served my bowl of chili with a smile
I said, it's been a year since I last saw you
Wonder how you'd like to share a few good miles?
Well, the justice of the peace was very sleepy
I held her in my arms the whole night long
I whispered words like 'settled down' and 'family'
And when I woke up my Calilou was gone

SMILIN' BILL McCALL

Well, the whole town listened to the radio
For the Smilin' Bill McCall show
Why, everyone in Nashville was listenin' to Bill

   'I don't want to be layin' in bed
   When they pronounce me dead.'

He'd stand and breathe in the microphone
With his guitar hangin' to his knee bone
All the girls would sit and dream
   When Bill began his theme

   'I don't want my hat to be hung
   When my last song is sung.'

But he never let fame go to his head
'This is Smilin' Bill McCall,' he said
'Gonna pick and sing a song or two
Y'all listen till I'm through.

   'And if you're at home at the house or in your car
   Tune in this time tomorrow.'

To all the boys he was the big hero
They'd glue their ears to the radio
Then talk in a most unusual drawl
   Imitatin' Bill McCall

   'Daddy, can I get me a guitar?
   Cause I want to be a star.'

The girls would say of Bill McCall
Why, I bet he's over six feet tall
Handsomest man in Nashville
They said of Smilin' Bill

'He won't be plantin' potater slips
When he cashes in his chips.'

Then one day Bill didn't make the show
Didn't even show up for a week or so
The station's boss said to City Hall,
    'Find Smilin' Bill McCall

    'It won't be hard to track him down
    He's got the biggest feet in town.'

Well, there's a creek that runs through Nashville
And on the bank they found Smilin' Bill

    He's committin' suicide
    But they grabbed him before he tried

'Turn me loose, I'm gonna jump,' he screamed
'Cause I can't stand that theme.

    'Let this be my final breath
    Cause I'm scared half to death.'

The big brave Smilin' Bill McCall
Is only four feet tall

    'I'd rather be in the river dead
    Than to hear 'em laughin' at my bald head'

JOHNNY CASH THE SONGS

ROCK 'N' ROLL RUBY

Well, I took my Ruby jukin' on the outskirts of town
She took her high heels off and let her stockin's down
She put a quarter in the jukebox to get a little beat
Everybody started watchin' all the rhythm of the feet

   She's my rock 'n' roll Ruby
   Rock 'n' roll
   Rock 'n' roll Ruby
   Rock 'n' roll
   When Ruby starts a-rockin'
   It satisfies my soul

Well, Ruby started rockin' 'bout a-one o'clock
And when she started rockin' she just couldn't stop
She rocked on the tables and she rocked on the floor
With everybody givin' Ruby rocked some more

It was round about four and I thought she would stop
She looked at me and then she looked at the clock
She said, 'Wait a minute, Daddy, now don't you get sore
All I want to do is rock a little bit more.'

One night my Ruby left me alone
I tried to contact her on the telephone
I finally found her about a-twelve o'clock
She said, 'Leave me 'lone, Daddy,
   Cause your Ruby wants to rock.'

FACE OF DESPAIR

Fingers calloused from the plow
Wrinkled weather-beaten brow
Streak of silver in the hair
    um mmm mmmm
    Face of despair

A back that's bent from years of toil
Thorns grow in the worn-out soil
No one left to really care
    um, um mmm mmmmmm
    Face of despair

If you should plow old fields like these
You'd plow up memories
Don't tell the young to mend their ways
You can't show them better days

Their better days are yet ahead
Your better days have long been dead
Rest easy in your rockin' chair
    um, mmm, mmmmmm
And look out at your September country
    Face of despair

Shoulders weary from the load
Life is as rough as a gravel road
How much of it can you bear?
    um mm mmm
Look at your September country
    Face of despair

In the September of your years
Eyes that hide a veil of tears
A look of longing always there
    um, um mmmm, mmmmm
    Face of despair

TIGER WHITEHEAD
(with N.T. Winston)

Wild black berries blooming in the thicket on the mountain
Sheepshire and watercress are growin' round the fountain
Where a big black bear is drinkin', lappin' water like a dog
Tiger Whitehead's in the bed, sleepin' like a log
But tomorrow he'll see bear tracks seven inches wide
And by sundown he'll be bringin' in the hide

Pretty Sally Garland comin' down the mountain side
Where Tiger Whitehead's grindin' at the mill, at the mill
She sits down on a bearskin and she says, you'll be my man
I'll have me the best bear hunter in these hills

A wild child was Tiger Whitehead and they say he killed
Ninety-nine bears before he went to rest, went to rest
Once he left two bear cubs orphaned
    But he brought 'em right on home
And Sally nursed the two bear cubs upon her breast

Tiger now is eighty-five and laid upon his bed
And the bears he killed now numbered ninety-nine,
    Ninety-nine
Some fellers trapped a bear but Tiger said
    'Just let him go
If he ain't runnin' wild, he won't be mine'

But at night when the wind howls
    'Cross the hills of eastern Tennessee
And when the lightnin' flashes there's a strange thing
    That people say they see
An old grey-headed ghost running through the mountains there
It's Tiger Whitehead after his one hundredth bear

I GOT A BOY
(and His Name Is John)

I got a boy and his name is John
You oughta see little John tag along
   Goin' where his Daddy goes
   Learnin' what his Daddy knows

We got a boy and his name is John
You oughta see little John tag along
   Goin' where his Daddy goes
   Learnin' what his Daddy knows

He's got a friend and her name is Kay
And Kay goes with him every day
   Gonna take Kay along
   Gonna teach Kay this song

He's got a friend and his name is George
But he's not the one from Valley Forge
   And he's never been president
   That ain't the George we meant

He's got a friend and his name is Gibbs
Gibbs is so fat you can't see his ribs
   A dog named Sergeant too, he's his friend
   Watch out he might bite you

I got a boy and his name is John
You oughta see little John tag along
   Goin' where his Daddy and Mommy goes
   Learnin' what his Daddy and Mommy knows

MISS TARA

Where are you goin'
   Miss Tara, Miss Tara?
Where are you goin'
   Miss Tara Jones?
Yesterday when you played
   On the swing and the trampoline
You were already thinkin'
   Of a life of your own
And I turned around twice
   And you're already gone

Who will you marry,
   Miss Tara, Miss Tara?
Who will you marry
   Miss Tara Jones?
Will he have wealth
   And will he have fame?
I'm sure too you're wonderin'
   Just who he will be
Well, that's your decision,
   It's not up to me

I hope you'll be happy,
   Miss Tara, Miss Tara
I hope you'll be happy,
   Miss Tara Jones
And that you will stay with me
   Till you're a woman
And wise to the world
   Before you're off on your own
You're my last baby girl
   And I'll be so alone

THE LITTLE MAN

It seems like some good people do get messed up
    On their chances
Ain't no doubt it's all been planned out
    Before they were born
Always goin' up that long downhill road
Always at the little end of the horn

Oh, the little man don't count
They look right over his head
And they turned him and they burned him
    Anyway they can
Just somebody's mean and closed
    Everybody's underdog
Oh, Heaven help cause no one else will
    The little man

It seems like people would get tired
    Of looking down on people
It seems like people got to have someone
    To kick around
Always feeling like they need to be looked up to
And always someone there when they look down

THE BALLAD OF ANNIE PALMER

On the island of Jamaica
Quite a long, long time ago
At Rose Hall plantation where the ocean breezes blow
Lived a girl named Annie Palmer
    The mistress of the place
And the slaves all lived in fear to see
    A frown on Annie's face

Where's your husband, Annie?
Where's number two and three?
Are they sleepin' 'neath the palms
Beside the Caribbean sea?
At night I hear you ridin'
And I hear your lovers call
And I still can feel your presence
Round the great house at Rose Hall

Well, if you should ever go to see
The great house at Rose Hall
There's expensive chairs and china
And great paintings on the wall
They'll show you Annie's sitting room
And the whipping post outside
But they won't let you see the room
Where Annie's husbands died

FOR THE COWBOY
(Jack Clement)

Some days are better than others
But sometimes he's the same, all the time
He's proud as Rockefeller's peacock
Even if he didn't have a dime

Just don't complain around him
You got no problem he ain't ever had
And just like anybody
He's part good and he's part bad

It's been fortune after fortune
That he gave away to his fellow man
He might be rich again tomorrow
But tomorrow give it all away again

He'll pay for your long distance
And he gives you all his cold drinks for free
So if you don't like the cowboy
Watch your mouth, when you mention him to me

He plays evangelical dobro
And soul-stirring slide guitar
He's a 'C plus' Christian
Somewhere between a black hole and a star
He stands at his window
And watches you come bringing in your song
But you're wasting his time
If they're not under three minutes long

He'll take a trip on polka
To carry himself to another scene
Sometimes he's melancholy
And his eyes get misty singing 'When I Dream'

He stood the test of time
That proves the good and worth of any man
Deceit and dishonesty are two words
That he doesn't understand

In any confrontation his shoulder's square
And again he's a Marine
With eyes that never waver
And a smile that could win a teenage queen

For years he went away
But no time at all had passed when he came back
He said, 'Hello, this is the Cowboy'
'Well, hi – be down first thing tomorrow, Jack'

He plays evangelical dobro
And soul-stirring slide guitar
He's a 'C plus' Christian
Somewhere between a black hole and a star
He stands at his window
And watches you come bringing in your song
But you're wasting his time
If they're not under three minutes long

CINDY, I LOVE YOU

We never really got right down to talkin'
We couldn't seem to find the place or time
Distance and the miles between us
    Made us kinda strangers
And it added to the distance already there
    Between our minds

And Cindy, I love you
    Yes, I love you
    Yes, I love you
And when I can't think of anything to say
Don't be readin' something in my mind
    That isn't there
Remember Cindy, I love you
     Anyway

I look at you and wonder what you're thinkin'
I'm sure you felt the same a time or two

We must both remember that true love
    Should cost us nothin'
You just owe me your affection
    And I owe the same to you

MUSIC

I HARDLY EVER SING BEER-DRINKING SONGS

I hardly ever sing beer-drinkin' songs
And when they play them cheatin' tunes
   I never sing along
I never sing the blues
I've forgotten 'Born to Lose'
And I hardly ever sing beer-drinkin' songs

I hardly ever walk the floor and cry
And I don't think I've ever said
   I feel like I could die
I don't' ever lay awake
I never think my heart will break
I hardly ever walk the floor and cry

I hardly ever sing beer-drinkin' songs
I can't put much feelin' in sayin'
   Love has all gone wrong
I don't lose no sleep at night
Cause things with you are goin' right
And I hardly ever sing beer-drinkin' songs

I never call your name out in my sleep
You never make me worry
   And you never make me weep
I never wonder if you're true
I spend the night curled up with you
And I never call your name out in my sleep

PLEASE DON'T PLAY RED RIVER VALLEY

Well, I see you got yourself a brand-new harmonica
Mail ordered from the Speigel catalog
Boy, I hope you can learn to play it like Lonnie Glosson
And while you're at it you oughta learn a verse or two of
    'Red River Valley',
    'Oh My Darlin' Clementine',
    or 'Salty Dog'

Oh, but please don't play 'Red River Valley'
How about 'Polly Wolly Doodle all day' in C?
You know, the only song I ever learned to play
    On my two-dollar-and-ninety-eight-cent harmonica
    That I got from Wayne Raney in Clint, Texas
    C-L-I-N-T Clint, Texas
    Was 'Red River Valley'
Then she said farewell to my French harp and me

Well, I see you're doin' pretty good on your new harmonica
But don't you think you oughta learn
    About one more tune, you know?
See, you hold it like you'se gonna eat a handful of popcorn
And sometimes you suck in and sometimes you blow

I WILL ROCK AND ROLL WITH YOU

They used to call me rockabilly
   All of us ran through
When Elvis opened up the door
   Bop-a-lop-bam-boo
I didn't ever play much rock and roll
Cause I got so much country in my soul
But I'm different man for lovin' you
And I'd take a shot at what you asked me to
And baby, I will rock and roll with you
   If I have to

Memphis nineteen-fifty-five on Union Avenue
Carl and Jerry and Charlie and Ray and Billy Riley too
A new sun risin' on the way we sing
And a world of weirdos waitin' in the wings
But I love you and though I'm past forty-two
There are still a few things I didn't do
And baby, I will rock and roll with you
   If I have to

I'M GONNA SIT ON THE PORCH
AND PICK ON MY OLD GUITAR

I'm gonna sit on the porch and pick on my old guitar
I'm gonna lay on my back and laugh at my lucky stars
And then I'm gonna fly away and never come back some day
'Less I thought I'd land right close to where you are
Well, if I thought anybody really cared I'd send back word
Strapped to the leg of a transcelestial bird
    I wonder if I ever really did leave
    How many would there be to grieve
How they'd react to the word

Well, I wouldn't want to hurt a solitary soul
I have still got all six-foot-two in control
    But when my obligations' load
    Is a greasy uphill road
And pleasin' everybody but me is my first goal

I want to sit on the porch and pick on my old guitar
And just hope you're hangin' loose wherever you are
    And for the joy you brought to me
    The song I sung for thee
While I sit on the porch and pick on my old guitar

LUTHER'S BOOGIE

We were just a plain ol' hillbilly band
With a plain ol' country style
We never played the kind of songs
That would drive anybody wild

We played a railroad song with a stompin' beat
We played a blues song, kinda slow and sweet
But the thing that knocked them off-a their feet
   Was ooh wee

When Luther played the boogie woogie
Luther played the boogie woogie
Luther played the boogie
In the strangest kind of way

Hear dear Luther play the boogie strange!

Well, we did our best to entertain everywhere we'd go
We'd nearly wear our fingers off
   Just to give the folks a show
We played the jumpin' jive to make 'em get in the groove
We played the sad songs, real slow and sweet
But the only thing that'd make them move was
When Luther played the boogie woogie

WHEN PAPA PLAYED THE DOBRO

My Papa was a hobo
When they delivered me
We didn't have the doctor
Cause he couldn't pay the fee
But when the goin' got too bad
To ease his misery
Papa played the dobro this-a way

Company would come around
He kept the dobro hid
He knew he couldn't play the way
The other players did
Why, the guitar's resonator
Was a gallon bucket lead
But Papa played the dobro this-a way

ROCKABILLY BLUES
(Texas 1955)

I took a tour to Texas
And from Waco I called you
But day by day no answer
And I'm Big Bluebonnet blue

I'm singing and they're dancing
But I'm feeling Big D bad
I'm Sweetwater beat
And I'm Texas City sad

The rhythm keeps me living
But have you heard the news?
There's a song singer coming
With rockabilly blues

It's hard to keep on singing
When you're lonesome to the bone
Ten thousand happy people
But I'm San Antone alone

One night stands and the man demands
That I get up and go
I'm Odessa desperate
And San Angelo low

It's the same old tune in Temple
About the loving I ain't had
I'm getting Beaumont bitter
And Amarilla mad

I'm giving up on calling you
Cause you're evading me
I'm coming home and if you're gone
I'm gonna be Tennessee free

ANOTHER SONG TO SING

Do they ask you where I am or where I've been?
Do they ever say, 'Where is the lonely friend?'
Is my name whispered in your bedside prayers?
Do you feel a vacant spot beside you there?

Well, there's always one more path that I must walk
And there's people I should sit down with and talk;
And somebody might appreciate the flowers I could bring
   So there's always another song to sing

Do you tell them I was wilder than the wind?
Do you remember that I needed lots of friends?
And at other times I'd rather be alone
   Where I could not be found when I was gone

Well, there's always one more canyon to explore
To touch the things left by those gone before
At the top of the tiniest hill I can feel like I'm a king
   And there's always another song to sing

TENNESSEE FLATTOP BOX

In a little cabaret
In a South Texas border town
Sat a boy and his guitar,
And the people came from all around
And all the girls from here to Austin
Were slippin' 'way from home
And puttin' jewelry in hock
To take the trip, to go and listen
To the little dark-haired boy that played
The Tennessee flattop box
   And he would play . . .

Well, he couldn't drive a wrangle,
And he never cared to make a dime;
But give him his guitar,
And he'd be happy all the time
And all the girls from nine to ninety
Were snappin' fingers, tappin' toes
And beggin' him, don't stop;
They were hypnotized and fascinated
By the little dark-haired boy that played
The Tennessee flattop box
   And he would play . . .

Then one day he was gone
And no one ever saw him 'round;
He vanished like the breeze
And they forgot him in the little town
And all the girls still dreamed about him
And they hung around the cabaret
Until the doors were locked;
And then one day, on the hit parade
Was a little dark-haired boy that played
A Tennessee flattop box.
   And he would play . . .

GET RHYTHM

Hey, get rhythm when you get the blues
Come on, get rhythm when you get the blues
Get a rock 'n' roll feeling in your bones
Put taps on your toes and get gone
Get rhythm when you get the blues

A little shoeshine boy he never gets low-down
But he's got the dirtiest job in town
Bending low at the people's feet
On a windy corner of a dirty street
Well, I asked him while he shined my shoes
How'd he keep from getting the blues
He grinned as he raised his little head
He popped his shoeshine rag and then he said:

Get rhythm when you get the blues
Come on, get rhythm when you get the blues
A jumpy rhythm makes you feel so fine
It'll shake all your trouble from your worried mind
Get rhythm when you get the blues

Well, I sat and I listened to the shoeshine boy
And I thought I was gonna jump for joy
Slapped on the shoe polish left and right
He took his shoeshine rag and he held it tight
He stopped once to wipe the sweat away
I said, 'You mighty little boy to be a-workin' that way'
He said, 'I like it' with a big wide grin
Kept on a-poppin' and he said again:

Get rhythm when you get the blues
Come on, get rhythm when you get the blues
It only cost a dime, just a nickel a shoe
It does a million dollars worth of good for you
Get rhythm when you get the blues

SING IT PRETTY, SUE

So you gave up all between us
For a glamorous career
And with all your talent you should be
The big star of the year
Then you'll be public property
So I release my claim to you
Go on and give 'em all you've got
   Sing it pretty, Sue

I can't take just part of you
And give the world a half
So smile for all the papers
And give 'em autographs
Go on to all the cities
So your public can see you
But I'll watch on television
   So sing it pretty, Sue

I hope you'll soon be on the top
Of every hit parade
I'll try to be excited
'Bout the progress that you've made
I'll collect your pictures
Like any fan would do
And I'll buy all your records
   So sing it pretty, Sue

But I won't ever tell a soul
That we have ever met
I'll just be one of millions
Who'll give the praise you get
And maybe every year or so
I'll drop a card to you
To tell you I'm still listening
   So sing it pretty, Sue

PLACES

THE WHIRL AND THE SUCK

It took a mighty good man with salty hands
And a mighty long raft to keep the fore before the aft
You take ten good men and guts and luck
And you might navigate the whirl and the suck

Well, the Tennessee River changed its mind
At Chattanooga she oughta unwind
She could-a turn right on to the Georgia Sea
But she cut right back through Tennessee

Well, the settlers came by raft and boat
Bringin' anything that would stay afloat
But like a loco horse that'll twist and buck
They hardly ever made it through the whirl and the suck

When General Washington was in his knickerbocks
The Cherokee Indians threw the Chattanooga Rocks,
And the Chickamauga Tribe and the Nickajack
Picked up the watch when the river cut back
And if a raft or a boat ever rode the bend
The Indians got 'em cause they had 'em hemmed in

FROM SEA TO SHINING SEA

RECITATION:

The beautiful spacious skies
The amber waves of grain
Through the majestic purple mountains
　　Above the fruited plain
God did shed his grace from sea to shining sea
　　On you and on me
From the Sleepy Hollow mountain country
To the swamps of Okefenokee to Guthrie, Oklahoma
　　To Hibbing, Minnesota
To Grant's Pass, Oregon to Stove Pipe Wells, California
　　From Texas to Montana
　　From California to Maine
In the sunny days, the winter snow
From Arizona sand to Cherokee, North Carolina
　　To Tarpan Springs, Florida
America, it's time to be refreshed,
　　Recalled to memory
God did shed his grace on thee
From sea to shining sea
　　The land is big,
　　The best is free
　　Sand and surf,
　　Grass and tree
From sea to shining sea

Past Virginia down from Maine
It's rolling, wild terrain
Three thousand miles of shore
Just like three thousand years before
Then the hills begin to rise
Till the almost touch the skies
From the flat black Delta land

To the singing Kansas sand
Down from the desert heat I see
Keeping it ours, forever free
    From sea to shining sea

GOING TO MEMPHIS

Bring a drink of water, Leroy
Bring a drink of water.
   'No!' Hm!
If I could get to the mercy man,
He'll give me some,
   I know, hm!

I got a gal in Vicksburg;
Bertha is her name, hm!
I wish I was tied to Bertha
Instead of this ball and chain

I'm goin' to Memphis, yes uh-huh
I'm goin' to Memphis, yeah

A dude took all my money;
Wouldn't let me see the cards. hm!
I owe the boss about a hundred years
For sleepin' in his back

Never been to Chicago,
But it must be a mighty fine place, hm!
I couldn't get past Tennessee
With Mississippi all over my face

Well, I'm goin' to Memphis, yes uh-huh
I'm goin' to Memphis, yeah

Well, a freezing ground at night
Is my old folding bed, hm!
Hope Saturday's my bread and meat,
And it will be till I'm dead

Well, I brought me a little water
In a Mister Prince Albert can, hm!
But the boss man caught me drinkin' it,
And I believe he broke my hand

Well, I'm goin' to Memphis,
    Yes, uh-huh
I'm goin' to Memphis,
    Yeah, I'm goin' to Memphis

They all call me crazy
For sassin' Mister Scott. Hm!
My brother was killed for a deed I did,
But I disremember what.

Well, another boy is down;
Shovel burned him out. Hm!
Let me stand on his body
To see what the shoutin's all about

Well, I'm goin' to Memphis,
    Yes, uh-huh,
I'm goin' to Memphis, yeah,
I'm goin' to Memphis

Hm! Like a bitter weed, I'm a bad seed
Cause when that levee's through and I am too,
Let the honky tonk roll on.
Come morning I'll be gone.
I'm goin' to Memphis

BIG RIVER

Now, I taught the weeping willow how to cry, cry, cry
And I showed the clouds how to cover up a clear blue sky
And the tears that I cried for that woman
   Are gonna flood you, Big River
Then I'm gonna sit right here until I die

I met her accidentally in St Paul, Minnesota
And it tore me up ev'ry time I heard her drawl,
   Southern drawl.
Then I heard my dream was back down steam
   cavortin' in Davenport.
And I followed you, Big River, when you called

Then you took me to St Louis later on, down the river
A freighter said she's been here but she's gone,
   Boy, she's gone.
I found her trail in Memphis,
   But she just walked up the bluff
She raised a few eyebrows and then she went on down alone.

Well now, I pulled into Natchez the next day, down the river
And there wasn't much there to make a rounder stay very long
And when I left it was raining so nobody saw me cry
Big River, why's she doing me that way?

Now, won't you batter down by Baton Rouge,
   River Queen, roll it on.
Take that woman on down to New Orleans, New Orleans
Go on, I've had enough; dump my blues down in the Gulf
She loves you, Big River, more than me

Now, I taught the weeping willow how to cry, cry, cry
And I showed the clouds how to cover up a clear blue sky
And the tears that I cried for that woman
    Are gonna flood you, Big River,
Then I'm gonna sit right here until I die

STRAWBERRY CAKE

In New York City just walkin' the street
Ran out of money, had nothing to eat
I stopped at the Plaza, that fancy hotel
Where you can check in if you're well-to-do well

The first of July and one hundred and four
I stopped at the Plaza's front revolving door
I stepped in the door and went around for a ride
Treating myself to the cool air inside
Then I found myself in a chandeliered room
Where people were dining and I hid in the gloom
My hunger pains hurt until I thought I would break
When a waiter brought out a big strawberry cake

Oh, that strawberry cake
Oh, that strawberry cake
Out in California them berries were grown
And into the city them berries were flown
For makin' that strawberry cake

Then I thought of Oxnard just north of LA
Where I picked strawberries for many a day
Hard work with no future, for the harvest was done
And I headed eastward a-travelin' by thumb
And nobody wanted me here in this town
I felt like a stray dog they all kick around
Them berries reminded me of my bad breaks
I'm hungry and I want that strawberry cake

I deserve that strawberry cake
Deserve that strawberry cake
I ran and I grabbed it and out the side door
Into Central Park through the bushes I tore
Holdin' my strawberry cake

I looked back behind me and what do I see?
The chef and headwaiter and the maitre d'
I had a nice helping of cake as I ran
I gobbled them berries as fast as I can
They're closin' the gap as I slowed down to eat
But the cake brought a new surge of power to my feet
I hid in the bush when the lead I did take
And I quietly finished my strawberry cake

I ate all that strawberry cake
That fine, fancy strawberry cake
Someone at the Plaza is without dessert
But for the first time in days now my belly don't hurt
I'm full of strawberry cake

DESTINATION VICTORIA STATION

I'm standing in the station
I'm looking at the board
The board ain't sayin' nothin'
That's lightenin' my load

Is your destination Victoria Station?
Where the trains go out and the trains come in
Where the trains go out and the trains come in

Her daddy's name was Casey
She lived down by the track
I know she was born to ramble
But I believe she'll ramble back

Destination Victoria Station
Where the trains go out and the trains come in
Where the trains go out and the trains come in

I asked an old conductor
Who just came in from the sea
Did you see a pretty little lady
Who looked like she missed me?

SHAMROCK DOESN'T GROW IN CALIFORNIA

Shamrock doesn't grow in California
And your shillaly is a forty-five
   It's the leaf of all the chiefs
   But I can't keep it alive
Cause shamrock doesn't grow in California

A letter came from my sweetheart in Ireland
The envelope was brimming full of tiny shamrock seeds
   She said, I'm sure you know
   You can't make this shamrock grow
Don't plant it over there beside the sage and jimson weed

Well, I planted the shamrock seeds my sweetheart sent me
'Me thumb is Irish green,' I said
   'For me they're sure to grow.'
   My good friend Mike O'Shay
   Came every day for thirty days
When cactus grew instead, Mike said
   'Well, I coulda told you so.
   Don't you know, boy, that
Shamrock doesn't grow in California?'

COMMITTED TO PARKVIEW

There's a man across the hall
Who sits staring at the floor
And he thinks he's Hank Williams
Hear him singing through the door

There's a girl in 202
Who stops to visit me
And she talks about her songs
And the star that she should be

There's a real fine talent
Stayin' in or passing through
And for one thing or another
They're committed to Parkview

There's a girl in 207
Coming down on florazine
And a superstar's ex-drummer
Trying to kick benzedrine

There's a real fine country singer
Who has tried and tried and tried
They just brought him in this morning
An attempted suicide

There are those who never made it
Those who did and now are through
Some came of their own good choosing
Some committed to Parkview

There's a girl who cries above me
Loud enough to wake the dead

They don't know what she has taken
That has scrambled up her head

There's a boy just down below me
Who's the son of some well-known
He was brought in by his mother
Cause his daddy's always gone

There's a bum from down on Broadway
And a few quite well-to-do
Who have withdrawn from the rat race
And committed to Parkview

They wake me about 6.30
Just before the morning meal
While they're taking my blood pressure
They ask me how I feel

And I always say fantastic
There ain't nothing wrong with me
And then they give me my injection
And I go right back to sleep

And my days are kinda foggy
And my nights are dreamy too
For they're taking good care of me
While committed to Parkview

DOWN AT DRIPPIN' SPRINGS

Campers, bikes, and mobile homes
Cars and pickup trucks
Shags and '59 hairdos
Sideburns, beards and ducks
There's Lone Star, Pearl and fried chicken
And one big cloud of smoke
Plug it in and turn it on
And the music goes for broke

Down at Drippin' Springs
Down at Drippin' Springs
There's Willie, Waylon, Kris and Tom
Have you heard Gatlin sing?
Down at Drippin' Springs
Down at Drippin' Springs

Duncan's on and Linda's next
How many did y'all bring?
Down at Drippin' Springs

Well, the Texas sun is low and hot
Upon the chaparral
It would be one ideal spot
For God to put his hell
The most beloved cowboy songs
That go across the plains
T. Texas Tyler ain't forgotten
Next year y'all come again

Down at Drippin' Springs
Down at Drippin' Springs
There's Russell, Bush, and Kris and Coe
Have you heard Gatlin sing?
Down at Drippin' Springs
Down at Drippin' Springs

Duncan's on and Rita's next
How many did y'all bring?
Down at Drippin' Springs

SATURDAY NIGHT IN HICKMAN COUNTY

When the sun goes down in Nashville
Go out that Memphis highway
Between Centerville and Dickson
On the gravel roads and byways
They'll be runnin' off the shine
That will be bringing in the bounty
Saturday night in Hickman County

At the beer joint on the blacktop
Country music's playing steady
And the working men are drinkin'
And they're rough and they are ready
And the girl behind the counter
Who has all the boys a-buzzin'
Will be leavin' with her husband
Saturday night in Hickman County

Down upon the Piney River
Parked beside the pretty waters
In the backseat of a Chevy
Is your next-door neighbor's daughter
They have split up into pairs
The four that went off datin' double
Gettin' that poor girl into trouble
Saturday night in Hickman County

All the farmers in the valley
Will be sittin' by the fire
Watch the late news on the TV
Then they'll quietly retire
Thankful just to be a-livin'
Thankful that tomorrow's Sunday
Sorry that the next day's Monday
Saturday night in Hickman County

IF IT WASN'T FOR THE WABASH RIVER

Fish ain't bitin'
But I don't really care
I'm in no hurry
Like that Wabash River there
I'd be drinkin' or layin' dead somewhere
If it wasn't for the Wabash River

If it wasn't for the Wabash River
And this willow tree and my pole and my line
I'd be goin' crazy as an Indiana cyclone
Drownin' memories of her and cryin'
   Cryin', cryin'
If it wasn't for the Wabash River
I'd be goin' out of my mind

It's so peaceful
Sittin' here beneath my tree
Lord, I need her like she often needed me
Life ain't worth it
Just as far as I can see
If it wasn't for the Wabash River

FORTY SHADES OF GREEN

I close my eyes and picture
The em'rald of the sea
From the fishing boats at Dingle
To the shores of Dunadee
I miss the River Shannon
And the folks at Skipparee
The moorlands and the midlands
With their forty shades of green

But most of all I miss a girl in Tipperary Town
And most of all I miss her lips as soft as eiderdown
Again I want to see and do
The things we've done and seen
Where the breeze is sweet as Shalimar
And there's forty shades of green

I wish that I could spend an hour
At Dublin's churning surf
I'd love to watch the farmers
Drain the bogs and spade the turf
To see again the thatching
Of the straw the women glean
I'd walk from Cork to Larne
To see the forty shades of green

SHANTYTOWN
(with June Carter)

I live down in Shantytown
Where chicken's twenty cents a pound
And if you live on such solid ground
Whatcha doin' down in Shantytown?
Whatcha doin' down in Shantytown?

Well, I'm back on your side of the tracks
Have you come back for me to take you back?
   Back to your high society
   To your cocktails and your teas
I'll look up, but don't look down
Cause we got pride in Shantytown

Behind the walls your shackled heart beats pure
While the rich have the love to endure
   Well, is the gold in your crown turning black?
   Is there something here in Shantytown
That keeps you comin' back?

Whatcha doin' down in Shantytown?

GROWING UP
COUNTRY

FIVE FEET HIGH AND RISING

How high is the water, Mama?
Two feet high and rising
How high is the water, Papa?
She said, it's two feet high and rising.
But we can make it to the road in a homemade boat
Cause that's the only thing we got left that'll float
It's already over the wheat and oats
Two feet high and rising

How high is the water, Mama?
Three feet high and rising
How high is the water, Papa?
She said, it's three feet high and rising.
Well, the hives are gone; I lost my bees;
Chickens are sleepin' in willow trees
Cows in water up past their knees
Three feet high and rising

How high is the water, Mama?
Four feet high and rising
How high is the water, Papa?
She said, it's four feet high and rising.
Hey, come look through the windowpane;
The bus is comin', gonna take us to the train.
Looks like we'll be blessed with a little more rain
Four feet high and rising

How high is the water, Mama?
Five feet high and rising
How high is the water, Papa?
She said, it's five feet high and rising.
Well, the rails are washed out north of town;
We gotta head for higher ground.
We can't come back till the water goes down
Five feet high and rising

GROWING UP COUNTRY

COUNTRY BOY

Country boy
Ain't got no shoes
Country boy
Ain't got no blues

Well, you work all day while you're wantin' to play
In the sun and the sand with a face that's tan
But at the end of the day when your work is done
    You ain't got nothin' but fun

Country boy
Ain't got no ills
Country boy
Don't owe no bills

You get a wiggly worm and then you watch him squirm
While you put him in on the hook
    And then you drop him in the brook
And if everything's gonna turn out right
    You're gonna fry fish tonight

Country boy
You're lucky free
Country boy
I wish I was you and you was me

Country boy
You got work to do
Country boy
In the morning dew

You gotta cut the weeds, you gotta plant the seeds
There's many a row you know you gotta hoe
But when it's quittin' time and your work is through
    There's a lotta life in you

JOHNNY CASH THE SONGS

Country boy
Got a shaggy dog
Country boy
Up the holler log

Well, he comes in a run when you pick up your gun
You get a shell or two and with your dog and you
When you get your rabbit you'll skin his hide
  He's gonna be good fried

Country boy
You got a lot to lose
Country boy
How I wish I was in your shoes

PICKIN' TIME

I got cotton in the bottom land
It's up and growin' and I got a good stand
My good wife and them kids of mine
Gonna get new shoes come pickin' time,
Get new shoes come pickin' time

Every night when I go to bed,
I thank the Lord that my kids are fed
They live on beans eight days in nine,
But I get 'em fat come pickin' time,
Get 'em fat come pickin' time

The corn is yellow and the beans are high
The sun is hot in the summer sky
The work is hard till layin' by,
Layin' by till pickin' time,
Layin' by till pickin' time

It's hard to see by the coal-oil light,
And I turn it off pretty early at night
Cause a jug of coal oil costs a dime
But I stay up late come pickin' time,
Stay up late come pickin' time

My old wagon barely gets me to town
I patched the wheels and I watered 'em down
Keep her in shape so she'll be fine
To haul my cotton come pickin' time,
Haul my cotton come pickin' time

Last Sunday morning when they passed the hat
It was still nearly empty back where I sat
But the preacher smiled and said, 'That's fine:
The Lord'll wait till pickin' time,
The Lord'll wait till pickin' time.'

JOHNNY CASH THE SONGS

THE MAN ON THE HILL

Will we get cold and hungry?
Will times be very bad?
When we're needing bread and meat
Where we gonna get it, Dad?
We'll get it from the man in the house on the hill
Yes, we will, from the man on the hill

Plowin' time is over
Still the fields are bare
How we gonna make a living
With twenty acres to share?
I'll beg for more land from the man on the hill
Yes, I will, I'll ask the man on the hill

I ain't got no Sunday shoes
That I can wear to town
Papa, reckon the boss has got
A pair of hand-me-downs?
I'll go and ask the man in the house on the hill
Yes, I will, I'll ask the man on the hill

Maybe he will help us
Maybe we'll get by
But who's gonna pay the dyin' bills
If we all should die?
We'll leave it to the man in the sky when we die
Yes, we'll leave it to the man in the sky

COUNTRY TRASH

I got a crib full of corn and a turnin' plow
But the ground's too wet for the hopper now
I got a cultivator and a double tree
And a leather line for the haw and gee
Let the thunder roll and the lightnin' flash
I'm doin' all right for country trash

I'm savin' up dimes for a rainy day
And I got about a dollar laid away
The wind's from the south and the fishin's good
Got a pot-bellied stove and a cord of wood
Mama turns the leftovers into hash
So I'm doin' all right for country trash

I got a mackinaw and a huntin' dog
And a cap that I ordered from the catalog
A big tall tree that shades the yard
And a big fat sow for the winter's lard
Let the thunder roll and the lightnin' flash
I'm doin' all right for country trash

Well, there's not much new ground left to plow
And crops need fertilizin' now
My hands don't earn me too much gold
For security when I grow old
But we'll all be equal when we're under the grass
And God's got a heaven for country trash

COTTON-PICKIN' HANDS
(with June Carter)

I'm a fair-to-middlin' man
These are cotton-pickin' hands
I'm a fair-to-middlin' man
And these are cotton-pickin' hands
My woman asks for little and nothing she demands
Except to hold these cotton-pickin' hands

The bloom is white and then it's red
Then it falls to leave a boll instead
The leaves fall and then it's white
We picked the pods from dawn to night

My woman cooks and sweeps the yard
And that old rough board's rough and hard
Her face is pretty though it's tan
And I love those cotton-pickin' hands

DON'T STEP ON MOTHER'S ROSES

We all were called to come back
To the old home on the farm
   Mother passed away
   What a mournful day
And as my daddy watched
His eyes were filled with pain and hurt
When someone stepped upon a rose
And crushed it in the dirt

Don't step on Mother's roses,
   Daddy cried
She planted them the day she was my bride
And every time I see a rose I see her smiling face
She made my darkest days look bright
   Round the old home place
Don't step on Mother's roses
   Let 'em grow
They way the did since many years ago
   They'll bloom for me each year
   And I'll have Mother near
Don't step on Mother's roses
   Let 'em grow

Years have passed away
And how the old home place has changed
   Daddy had to go
   We all miss him so
Children picked the roses
As they go along the way
But when their petals are abused
I hear my Daddy say
Don't step on Mother's roses
Let 'em grow

274

MOUNTAIN LADY

Mountain lady
Do you sit on your front porch
In the cool of the day?
Mountain lady
Did you think your kids
Would ever come back to stay?
Mountain lady
Does the columbine
Still twine around your door
And did you ever get a rug
To cover the cracks
Where my diaper drug on your wooden floor?

Oh, you Appalachian lady
Once I was your little baby
And you rocked me
   In your homemade rocking chair
Since I heard the wild goose callin'
I have done a lot of fallin'
Mountain Lady
Someday I'll come to you there

Mountain lady
Does the country church bell
Ring on Sunday morn?
Mountain lady
Do you still wear that ole apron
Ragged and torn?
Mountain Lady
On winter nights before our old fireplace
As you look into the flame
Do you ever call my name
And do you see my face?

NO, NO, NO

MALE:
I'm a poor boy from the farm land
Your father is a wealth sailin' man
   If I asked you for your hand
   Would you tell me
   No, oh, no, no, no?

FEMALE:
You're a poor boy from the farm land,
My daddy is a wealthy sailin' man
He told me if you asked me for my hand.
I'd better tell you
   No, oh, no, no, no

MALE:
Your daddy brings you silk to sew
From the finest shops in Tokyo
He told you to turn me down, I know
But don't say
   No, oh, no, no, no

FEMALE:
Yes, Daddy owns a clipper ship
And he brings me beads on every trip
And pink champagne for me to sip
And you're the poorest boy I know
   So no, no, no

MALE:
I can't give you anything
I can't afford a wedding ring
A present that I'd like to bring
But oh, I love you so,
   Oh, don't say no

276

FEMALE:

My daddy's three days out to sea

And he would turn me across his knee

If he knew you were kissing me

But I can't let you go

    Oh, no, no, no, oh

BOTH:

    No, no, no

TRAVELLIN'

THIS TOWN

This town ain't for me
I won't be stayin' round
This town is hard and cold
I'm not happy in this town

I'll pick up my heart and I'll go
Where to, I don't care or know
Don't matter where I'll be bound
As long as I leave this town

This town don't need me now
I'll soon be outward bound
This town don't want me here
And God, I don't want this town

Tomorrow who'll remember I came?
Tomorrow who'll remember my name?
Don't care which road I go down
As long as I eave this town
'Long as I leave this time
I've got to leave this town

WIDE OPEN ROAD

Well, you said you had enough
You said that you were leaving
I said, 'Shove off, honey'
Baby, I ain't grieving
Pack your bags and pull out this evening
    There's a wide open road

Early this morning
You were nowhere about
And so I searched the town
    But you had done pulled out
I looked north, east and west
And then a-leading south
    I saw a wide open road

There's a wide open road
It's leading south from my abode
    If you stick around
    And turn your damper down
There's a wide open road

Well, the reason I was lookin'
For you all over town
Was to tell you that your kitty kat
    Is still around
And you left your wedding ring
When you went down
    That wide open road

If you're gonna stay away
Then, honey, let me know
How to cook hot biscuits
    How to roll the dough
Everything's gone crazy since I told you to go
    Down the wide open road

There's a wide open road
And, honey, I want you to know
You can look down south
Or you can turn back home
    And there's a wide open road

ROLLIN' FREE

Rollin' free
Rollin' free
Rollin' free
Just the sun
   and the wind
   and the road and me
I don't want to be tied to a load
That I can't carry over the road
Just want to hear that thunder roar
On trails that ain't been rode before
   Don't put no chains on me
   I'm rollin' free

Now I'm worried about who I am
Cause frankly I don't give a damn
Long as I can be where I want to be
And doin' what I want to do
And if it's all the same to you
   What I want to be is rollin' free

Now I forgot about yesterday
And let tomorrow bring what may
Let everything be as it will be
Cause all I need is my machine
And a little high octane gasoline
And get your hands off me
   I'm rollin' free

HIT THE ROAD AND GO

I woke up this afternoon
And looked into your eyes
And something was as wrong
As if the sun forgot to rise
I picked up a road map
And I checked a few good places that I know
And if you're no longer givin'
I believe I'll hit the road and go

I just got the feelin'
That the fire was burnin' out
Cause the air was turnin' colder
Every time you came about
And the flame won't take a fannin'
If the last reserve of love is runnin' low
So since I've got a button-up
I believe I'll hit the road and go

County road 640, state highway 45
Life out off the interstate
    Is very much alive
There's magic in the mountains
And music in the valleys down below
And my song ain't through playin' yet
So I believe I'll hit the road and go

Good morning to you, sunshine
Good morning to you, rain
The windshield wipers' rhythm
Keeps me singing down the pain
Today I'm gonna miss you less
If I miss you at all you'll never know,
    You'll never know
The rambler has cut all the ties
And pulled up stakes to hit the road and go

TELL HIM I'M GONE

You take this hammer
Take it to the Cap'n
Hey, take this hammer
Take it to the Cap'n
Take this hammer
Take it to the Cap'n
You can tell him I'm gone
Tell him I'm gone

Cause I ain't gonna take
No more kicks and whippin's
No, I ain't gonna take
No kicks and whippin's
I ain't gonna take no more
No more of his kicks and his whippin's
You can tell him I'm gone, gone, gone
You can tell him I'm gone

Cap'n called me a hard-headed Devil
Well, the Cap'n called me
A hard-headed Devil
Well, the Cap'n called me
A hard-headed Devil
And that ain't my name
That ain't my name

Well, the Cap'n got a big gun
'Bout a ninety-nine calibre
Whoa, Cap'n got a big gun
'Bout a ninety-nine calibre
Well, the Cap'n got a big gun
About a ninety-nine calibre
He gonna shoot me down if he ever catches me
Gonna shoot me down

But you can tell him that I went
Where the grey goose goes
Tell him that I'm gone
Where the grey goose goes
Tell him I'm gone
Where the grey goose goes
Tell him I'm gone, but tell him I'm gone
Just tell him I'm gone

HUNGRY

Grit my teeth and face a new day dawning
Take a deep breath, then get up and go
   Tie the same ole weary shoes
   And walk the same ole pathway
I never see a face that I don't know
Oh, God, if I could just pack up and go

Hungry for some other face
Hungry for some other place
Needin' something and I know what
   God, I know what
I'm tired of seein' the same ole road
Tired of carryin' the same ole load
Hungry for something I ain't got

Her face across that table every mornin'
And lately I don't notice that she's there
   Always leave that breakfast table
   Feelin' so damned empty
She knows there's something wrong
   But I don't care
Oh, God, how much more of this can I bear?

LOVE GONE RIGHT

I WALK THE LINE

I keep a close watch on this heart of mine
I keep my eyes wide open all the time
I keep the ends out for the tie that binds
    Because you're mine
    I walk the line

I find it very, very easy to be true
I find myself alone when each day is through
Yes, I'll admit that I'm a fool for you
    Because you're mine
    I walk the line

As sure as night is dark and day is light
I keep you on my mind both day and night
And happiness I've known proves that it's right
    Because you're mine
    I walk the line

You've got a way to keep me on your side
You give me cause for love that I can't hide
For you I know I'd even try to turn the tide
    Because you're mine
    I walk the line

YOU DREAMER YOU
(also known as 'Oh, What a Dream')

I dreamed I walked in a field of flowers
    Oh, what a dream
The houses all were silver towers
    Oh, what a dream
Beside the road an angel sat,
I said hello and tipped my hat
And stopped when I saw her smile
And set me down a while
I set me down a while
    You dreamer you

I tried the angel for a kiss
    Oh, what a dream
But she turned away and my lips missed
    Oh, what a dream
She said, 'Sir, I'll have you know
I met you just a while ago
You're welcome for to sit
But calm yourself a bit, sir
Calm yourself a bit
    You dreamer you

I fell in love like one, two, three
    Oh, what a dream
I asked the angel to marry me
    Oh, what a dream
She said, 'Sir, I can't marry you,
But I'm a dream that can come true
There are dreams of much my worth
That live upon the earth, sir
Live upon the earth
    You dreamer you'

Then I awoke and found my love
    Oh, what a dream
As heavenly as the one above
    Oh, what a dream
We'll marry in a sea of flowers
Home will be a silver tower
There'll be heaven in my life
With an angel for a wife
With an angel for a wife
    You dreamer you
    You dreamer you

LOVE GONE RIGHT

FLESH AND BLOOD

Beside a singin' mountain stream
    Where the pussy willow grew;
Where silver leaf of maple sparkled
    In the morning dew
I braided twigs of willow,
Made a string of buckeye beads;
But flesh and blood needs flesh and blood
    And you are what I need
Flesh and blood needs flesh and blood
    And you are what I need

I leaned against a bark of birch
    And I breathed the honey dew;
Saw a northbound flock of geese
    Against the sky of baby blue,
Among the lily pads I carved a whistle from a reed
Wild honeysuckle vine is sweet
    But you are what I need
Honeysuckle vine is sweet
    But you are what I need

A mocking bird sang just for me
    And I thanked him for the song;
Then darkness floated up the hill
    And I had to move along.
Those are a few little things
On which the mind and spirit feed
But flesh and blood needs flesh and blood
    And you are what I need
Flesh and blood needs flesh and blood
    And you are what I need

YOU BEAT ALL I EVER SAW

I walked through every town
Saw fortunes lost and found
And when your trail failed
Walked holes in both my soles
But I don't expect you back
You're somewhere makin' tracks
I crossed your burnin' bridges
And walked through miles of sand
Met the lawless and the law
But you beat all I ever saw

I dreamed a million miles
About your eyes and smiles
And since I loved you the very best
I could turn from all the rest
And I'd scanned the skies for you
But I only saw your hue
They had thrown away your mould
You were made of frozen gold
And your heart would never thaw
You beat all I ever saw

You're the only light
That can pierce my ball of night
It comes from wantin' you
And breaks my will in two
I try to turn away
When there dawns a newborn day
But I can't lose your memories
You haunt my brightest hour
And you break me like a straw
You beat all I ever saw

I'D RATHER HAVE YOU

I'd rather go to a rodeo
Than shopping on Rodeo Drive
I'd rather lay on the grass with you
And watch the planes than to have to fly
   I'd rather have you
Than Ringling and Barnum and Bailey circus
With all three rings and the high trapeze
The lady on the horse
And the train that carries them through
Stacked up on the Golden African

I'd rather share a hot dog with you
Than dinner with the president
Offer me a castle on a mountaintop
   I'll take you in a tent
I'd rather be alone with you
Than to have my very own satellite
To talk and sing and say everything to everybody
   Do whatever I want to do
And be number one on *Who Is Who*
   I'd rather have you

I don't crave applause or praise
Or holidays with my way paid
I don't want to incorporate
Nor to be top rate nor a head of state
I don't want to play the digaree-do
Nor the sitar or the kazoo
Just the two of us alone will do
   I'd rather have you

I'd rather have tickets to the movies with you
Than the one that wins the lottery
Rather walk on the beach with you

Than to own all the ships at sea
I'd rather have you than the *QE2* and the Eiffel Tower,
   The Royal Jewels
And the Brooklyn Bridge and the toll paid to go through
And throw in a Texas well or two
   I'd rather have you

ALL OVER AGAIN

Every time I look at you I fall in love
    All over again
Every time I think of you it all begins
    All over again
One little dream at night
    And I can dream all day
It only takes a memory to thrill me
One little kiss from you
    And I just fly away
Pour me out your love until you fill me

I want to fall in love beginning from the start
    All over again
Show me how you stole away my heart
    All over again

COME IN, STRANGER

She said: 'Come in, stranger.
It's good to have you home.
   I hurried through
   Cause I knew it was you
   When I saw your dog waggin' his tail.
Honey, why didn't you let me know by mail?
You've been gone so long.'

She said: 'Come in, stranger.
I know you're weary from all the miles.
   Just sit right there
   In your easy chair
   And tell me all about the places you've been,
How long it'll be before you leave again?
I hope it's a long, long while.'

She said: 'Come in, stranger,
Everything 'round home is fine.
   I've watched and I've waited
   For you to get back
   And I missed you all the time.'

She said: 'Come in, stranger.
Oh, how I need you when you're gone.
   I walk the floor
   And I watch the door
   And then I lie awake and wonder where you can be.
I'd give anything to have you here with me.
I get so lonesome all alone.'

She said: 'Come in, stranger,
And won't you listen to my plea?
   Stay long enough
   So that the one I love
Is not a stranger all the time.'

WHAT DO I CARE

When I'm all through,
If I haven't been
   What they think I could be,
If the total isn't high enough
   When they figure me,
When I grow old if there's no gray
From worry in my hair
   What do I care?
   What do I care?

What do I care just as long
As you are mine a little while.
When the road was long and weary
You gave me a few good miles.
What do I care if I miss a goal
   Because I make a slip?
I'll still be satisfied because I tasted
   Your sweet lips

What do I care if I never have much money?
   And sometimes my table looks a little bare.
   Anything that I may miss
Is made up for each time we kiss
You love me and I love you,
   So what do I care?

JOHNNY CASH THE SONGS

I'M ALRIGHT NOW

I've been a rambler
I've been a gambler
I've been in trouble a time or two
I known a lot of good lookin' women
But, Lord, I blessed the day I found you

I'm alright now
I'm alright now
I was ridin' on the Devil's train
But I got off somehow
I'm alright now
I'm alright now
Gabriel, let your trumpet blow
I'm alright now

I've been demented
Been discontented
I've been in jail pretty close to hell
I've been frisky
On sippin' whiskey, yea
And I done a few other things
That I'll never tell

DRINK TO ME

A rose, a carnation, the lily and an orchid
Make such a pretty bouquet
But only the orchid was worthy of you
So I threw all the others away

Then you took the orchid and you breathed on its petals
And after a day or two
The flower still blooms but the scent's not the orchid's
It carries the savor of you

So if you're gonna drink to me
  Drink with your eyes
    And I'll never cry for wine
Or leave a kiss in an empty coffee cup
Then pass it from your lips to mine

Cause I've got a thirst burning way down in my soul
And honey from a sugar tree
Is not half as sweet as the air you breathe
Honey, come here and drink to me

W-O-M-A-N

I just want to tell you, baby, if I can
I need my W-O-M-A-N
A M-A-N needs a W-O
For love or dirty boogie or the do-se-do
And the F-E-M-A-L-E can
Turn a B-O-Y into a M-A-N

Well, I can take a failure, I can take a flop
I've survived at the bottom better than the top
I take it day by day, and I can do alright
If my W-O-M-A-N is in at night
I'm not talking good or bad, or lust or sin
Whoa, I'm just talking W-O-M-A-N

I can get along without a dog or a cat
And luxury is not where happiness is at
I can do without tobacco, coffee or tea
And I turn down lots of money making deals offered me
I can make it through the hills without a jeep or a van
But I gotta have my W-O-M-A-N

I need you woman
W-O-M-A-N, man, man
I need you and I'll keep you
Just as long as I can
Cause you are my W-O-M-A-N

I'LL SAY IT'S TRUE

I've never been in prison
I don't know much about trains
My favorite singer cooks my breakfast
I like her fancy and I like her plain
I love bright and flashing colors
Like hot pink and Dresden blue
But if they ask me if it's true
    That I still love you
    I'll say it's true

I'd be happy in a mansion
Or in an old rundown shotgun shack
I like the feel of silk and satin
So I don't know why I wear black
I love New York City
Bet your cowgirl boots I do
But if they ask me if it's true
    That I still love you
    I'll say it's true

I'll say it's true
So don't let it bother you
Just let them old tales all stay twisted
I will set 'em straight about you

I have not been in the Army
I'm an Indian from years ago
When they ask if I know Waylon
I tell 'em, 'I think so.'
I do not plan on retiring
From anything I do
But if they ask me if it's true
    That I still love you
    I'll say it's true

I got plans to keep right on singing
And I do know Emmylou
But if they ask me if it's true
   That I love you
   I'll say it's true

I'LL REMEMBER YOU

Come to me, sweetheart, and let me hold you
One minute more will help me through
    The loneliness that's due
Give me another kiss that I can dream on
Then you'll know that where I go
    I'll remember you

Hold my hand and tell me that you love me
Look at me the same old way as only you can do
    And when you're out of reach
My heart will know what to turn to
When you remember me remember,
    I'll remember you

I'll remember you
I'll remember you
    Honey, how could I forget
    When I love you
I'll remember you

You don't have to worry
    I'll remember you
    I'll remember you
Honey, how could I forget when I love you
    I'll remember you

KENTUCKY STRAIGHT

I've rambled 'round the countryside
I've drifted near and far
I've been off to seek my fortune
I've been following every star

I rode the Devil's highway
The hell-bound interstate
But now I'm back at happy shack
With my Kentucky straight

And we rise up every mornin' with the chickens
And every minute we're alive we're livin'
   She's a little bit old-fashioned
   But her lovin's up-to-date
And I'm happy here with my Kentucky straight

I had looked for satisfaction in the arms of quite a few
And I've done everything that was big enough to do
   But everywhere I'd see her face
   From Maine to Golden Gate
But I knew this was where it's at
   With my Kentucky straight

And we rise up every mornin' with the chickens
And every minute we're alive we're livin'
   I love her so she knows
   That it was worth her while to wait
Cause I'm happy here with my Kentucky straight

YOU'VE GOT A NEW LIGHT SHINING IN YOUR EYES

You've got a new light shining in your eyes
And I can see now right where your beauty lies
    And it's showin' in your face
    That your heart has found a place
And I can hear it in your whisper and your sighs

You're got a new way of doin' things you do
And it's plain to see there's been a change in you
    And I wonder could it be
    That the change is due to me
For I have felt a certain something too

You've got a way about you now
That you never had before
    You've got a look you're wearin' now
    Like no look you ever wore before
You tried to hide it for a while but now I realize
You've got a new light shinin' in your eyes

You've got a new light shinin' in your eyes

YOU REMEMBERED ME

You were young and needed love
And I was wild and free
But every time you said a prayer
You said a prayer for me

By the ring upon your hand
   We vowed fidelity
There were times when I forgot
   But you remembered me

You remembered only
That wedding bells would ring
You remembered only
To count the days till spring
You were filled with love and honor
But I couldn't see

I believed that promises
Were made to break apart
But every time I broke a vow
I always broke your heart

So here's to you; God bless you now
Wherever you may be
I regret that I forgot
Cause you remembered me

LOVE GONE RIGHT

RUN SOFTLY BLUE RIVER

Run softly, Blue River,
My darlin's asleep
Run softly, Blue River,
Run cool and deep
Oh, I thrill to her kisses
And she thrills to mine
Run softly while she sleeps
And dreams for a time

Cause she dreams of tomorrow
When she'll be my wife
And I pray that as peaceful
As you is our life
And if your murmuring soothes me
Till I'm sleeping too
Run softly, Blue River,
We'll both dream with you

HAPPINESS IS YOU
(with June Carter)

Way down the mountain
I chased a moonbeam
On the beach I built sandcastles too
   My moonbeams faded
   My castles tumbled
All of this was meaningless
   Cause happiness is you

I tried to doubt you
And live without you
Tried to deny that I love you like I do
   But I realize now
   And I'll admit it
You'll always be part of me
   Cause happiness is you

No more chasin' moonbeams
Or catchin' falling stars
I know now my pot of gold
Is anywhere you are
   My heart won't miss you
   My heart goes with you
Loneliness is emptiness
   But happiness is you

CAUSE I LOVE YOU

I'll sweep out your chimney,
Yes, and I will bring you flowers,
Yes, and I will do for you most anything
    You want me to;
If we live in a cottage,
You will feel like it's a castle
By the royal way you're treated
    And the attention shown to you;

I'll be there beside you,
If you need a crying shoulder;
Yes, and I'll be there to listen,
    When you need to talk to me;
When you wake up in the darkness,
I will put my arms around you,
And hold you till the morning sun
    Comes shinin' through the trees;

I'll be right beside you,
No matter where you travel,
I'll be there to cheer you
    Till the sun comes shinin' through;
If we're ever parted
I will keep the tie that binds us,
I'll never let it break
Cause I love you

I will bring you honey
From the bee tree in the meadow,
And the first time there's a rainbow
    I'll bring you a pot of gold
I'll take all your troubles
And I'll throw 'em in the river,
Then I'll bundle down beside you
    And I'll keep you from the cold

I'll be right beside you,
No matter where you travel,
I'll be there to cheer you
  Till the sun comes shinin' through;
If we're ever parted
I will keep the tie that binds us,
I'll never let it break
  Cause I love you

LOVE GONE RIGHT

YOU'RE THE NEAREST THING TO HEAVEN
(with Jimmy Atkins and Hoyt Johnson)

I have sailed the peaceful waters
Of the ocean deep and blue
I help my breath and watched
The western sunset's golden hue
I've flown above the mountain peaks
And valleys wide and green
But you're the nearest thing to heaven
    That I've seen

You're the nearest thing to heaven,
    Yes, you are
I have searched for happiness so long and far
    But my search for love was through
    The day that I found you
Cause you're the nearest thing to heaven,
    Yes, you are

I confess that I've been tempted
By alluring magic charms
When a smile was flashed my way
And stood before two open arms
But I turn and walk away
Because I love you like I do
You're the nearest thing to heaven,
    Darling, you

I have watched the silver raindrops
Fall to earth to cool the day
Watched the rainbow at twilight
When the clouds had blown away
I love the pretty flowers
Money cannot buy their worth
But you're the nearest thing to heaven
    On this earth

MY TREASURE

I saved a lot of money
My fortune was untold
And like a fool I idolized
My silver and my gold
My earthly treasures mounted
But when I counted through
I realized the treasure I had overlooked
    Was you

My treasure,
    Unmeasured
But forsaken of the treasures
That come from above
My treasure
    Unmeasured
But it don't hold the heart
    of the one that I love

If I had my life before me
If I could see it all
I'd stake my claim on things
That are secured against downfall
I'd work for earthly treasures
Like any man would do
But I'd set my sights much higher
And I'd be sure that I had you

STRAIGHT A'S IN LOVE

Well, a-readin' and a-writin' and a-rithmetic
Never did get through to me
It ain't because I'm square and thick
Cause I learned my ABC's
But when I graduated from the grammar school
And I moved one grade above
I began to be a snook at book
But I made straight A's in love

Now the teacher would say to learn your algebra
But I'd bring home C's and D's
How could I make an A
When there's a swingin' maid
On the left and on the right
And in the back and the front of me?

Oh, my grades are low on my card, I know
But they ought to give me one above
   If they'd give me a mark
   For learnin' in the dark
I'd have straight A's in love

Now in my senior year with graduation near
I did my homework every night
And when my Mama said I ought to go to bed
I'd turn out all the lights
But my sweetie pie was waitin' right outside
She'd be a-cooin' like a dove
   So I did my best
   I failed some master test
But I made straight A's in love

THE BABY IS MINE

Now, don't laugh at the condition the lady's in
She soon could wear a cocktail dress again
But we get along without cocktails mighty fine
This will be our first and I'm proud the baby is mine

Yes, I married her although I knew
The kind of life she used to live
And cause I knew she loved me too
   It was easy to forgive
And if you'd just mind your own business we'd be fine
Don't ever doubt I'm proud the baby is mine

She's awkward, yea, but have you seen her face?
Where there once was shame, there's sparkle in its place
And her conscience is clear, that's why her eyes shine
Mister, don't ever doubt, I'm proud the baby is mine

I married her although I knew
The kind of life she used to live
And cause I knew she loved me too
   It was easy to forgive
And if you'd just mind your own business we'd be fine
Tell all her old friends I'm proud the baby is mine

YOU'RE MY BABY
(also known as 'Little Woolly Booger')

Hey, I love that hair, long and black
Hanging down in the middle of your back
Don't you cut it off, whatever you do
Cause I need it to run my fingers through

Cause you're my baby
Uh huh, and my sugar
Don't mean maybe
Little woolly booger

Hey, I got a guitar, got six strings
And a guitar pick that'll make 'em ring
Every string's got a note or two
That I'm gonna use to serenade you

Well, I got a dollar that I saved
I saved it up for a rainy day
Everybody's calling for bills that's due
But if they don't catch me, I'll spend it on you

Well, I had me a gal, she said she's mine
But she run around on me all the time
Now she's gone and I'm glad we're through
Cause I'm plum goggle-eyed over you

Cause you're my baby
Uh huh, and my sugar
Oh, you drive me crazy
Little woolly booger

LOVE GONE WRONG

UNDERSTAND YOUR MAN

Don't call my name out your window,
   I'm leavin'
I won't even turn my head
Don't send your kinfolks to give me no talkin'
   I'll be gone, like I said

You'd say the same old things
That you been saying all along
Lay there in your bed and keep your mouth shut
   Till I'm gone
Don't give me that old familiar cryin' cussin' moan
   Understand your man
Tidy your bad mouth
   And understand your man

You can give my other suits to the Salvation Army
   And everything else I leave behind
I ain't takin' nothin' that'll slow down my travelin'
   While I'm untanglin' my mind

I ain't gonna repeat what I said anymore
While I'm breathin' air that ain't been breathed before
I'll be gone as a wild goose in winter
   Then you'll understand your man
   Meditate on it,
   Understand your man

I'M LEAVING NOW

Hold on, honey, I would like to say
I'm bustin' out and breakin' away
I'm lettin' you go like a hot horseshoe
I can't take another heartache from you

Think about how it's gonna be
When you start back to needin' me
When your dancin' shoes have lost their shine
I'm gonna be gone in mine

   I'm leavin' now
   I'm leavin' now
   Get outta my space,
   Get outta my face
   I'm leavin' now
   Hey, oh, I'm leavin' now

The time may come you have to trim the fat
Feed kitchen scraps to your front-seat cat
Bye bye, baby, when the bills come due
You may have to give up a jewel or two

Eat your heart out anyway
It's hard as your head and cold as clay
It's all over now, you won't have me
For your sugar daddy and your money tree

Turn up the collar on my travelin' coat
Sell that miserable pleasure boat
I wouldn't give a dime for another buck
I'm livin' on muscle, guts and luck

If anybody asks where did I go
Tell 'em I went where the wild goose goes
I won't even have an area code
Ain't no numbers on freedom road

A CERTAIN KIND OF HURTIN'

I've got a certain kind of hurtin' since you've gone
I've got a pain I can't explain
   And it keeps on hangin' on
You were gone one morning and I held on tight
But I went all to pieces later on that night
I got a certain kind of hurtin' since you've gone

I got a tear that's very near to showin' through
I get too weak to speak when I think of losing you
   You never got out of sight to my view
But nothing's gonna ever be right without you
I got a certain kind of hurtin' since you've gone

I've got a lonely heart that only beats for you
I hope you find I'm on your mind
   Needin' me like I need you
You're not leavin' on a one-way track
Cause I'm gonna come get you and I'm bringin' you back
I've got a certain kind of hurtin' since you've gone

I STILL MISS SOMEONE
(with Roy Cash Jr)

At my door the leaves are falling
The cold wild wind will come
Sweethearts walk by together
And I still miss someone

I go out on a party
And look for a little fun
But I find a darkened corner,
Cause I still miss someone

Oh, I never got over those blue eyes;
I see them everywhere
I miss those arms that held me
When all the love was there

I wonder if she's sorry
For leaving what we'd begun
There's someone for me somewhere,
And I still miss someone

LATELY

Lately I've been thinkin'
That you don't love me at all
Lately I've been reading
And the writing on the wall is saying
   Looks like you'll be going
   And I've no sure way of knowing
But somehow that's what I've been thinking
   Lately

Lately you've been saying things that I don't understand
Lately you look through me as if I'm another man
   Instead of your one and only
   I'm beginning to get lonely
I've been feeling you'll be leaving
   Lately

You might as well just stop it now
Cause I already know
You wouldn't hurt me less
If you'd just go ahead and go
   You know your heart's already gone
   So you might as well go on
Things have not been working for us
   Lately
Things have not been working for us
   Lately

HURT SO BAD

I thought I could walk away
And keep on goin'
Leave you flat and never once be sad
I didn't know the pain
Would keep on growin'
And I didn't know that it could hurt so bad
    Hurt so bad,
    Hurt so bad

All night long I'm out a-driving round
Every this 'n' that a-way like mad
Always end up on your side of town
I didn't know that it could hurt so bad
    Hurt so bad,
    Hurt so bad

Don't give in, go on
And don't look back
Hold on to my pride, I said
I won't let my heart turn my head

New day dawnin' on your world without me
You won't miss something that you never had
You'll be making it all right without me
But I didn't know that it could hurt so bad
    Hurt so bad,
    Hurt so bad

SHE'S A GO-ER

Well, I think that I should tell you she's a go-er
And when she goes she won't come back no more
There ain't nothing like it when you've got her all alone
And there's not anything that can replace her
    When she's gone
I envy you until the day she walks back out your door
And that she's gonna do,
    Cause she's a go-er

Now don't let her stay too long
She'll take the heart right out of your song
You'll pay the price for her one time
But she won't be back anymore
I just thought I'd tell you,
    She's a go-er

Yes, I guess I should have told you she's a go-er
I should have told you that way back long before
But I was trying to overcome the pain she put me through
I was fighting to forget her when she got around to you
You'll be heaven high till she don't want you anymore
Then she'll be gone again,
    Cause she's a go-er

THE WIND CHANGES

Yes, the wind changes and one morning early
A good wind'll be blowing for me
Yes, the wind changes and one morning early
A good wind'll be blowing for me

Away like a bird you have flown
And upon a wild wind you were blown
    Where you're bound, I don't know
    Nor the way that you go
But the wanderlust beckons you on

The wind sings its song in the tree
But the wind's song is never for me
    When following your track
    The wind's at your back
Making whirlwinds where you used to be

The wind quietly hides in the night
And it rises again with the light
    But the days never fly
    They're slow to go by
And, like you, they're something I can't fight

JOHNNY CASH THE SONGS

TIME AND AGAIN
(with June Carter)

I wish my heart was stone
Cause you're hard on flesh and bone
But even if my heart was stone
I couldn't stand it long

Cause time and time again
You're gone with the wind
And even when you're here I know
You're making plans to go

You come back and I take you back
But you're like the shifting sand
And, like the sand, you sift right through my hands
Time and time again, I got you
   Time and time again

I want to be your man
So I give in all I can
And when I give all I can, I give up
   Time and time again

You take hold of my hand
And I look at where I stand
And I say this is my last stand
   Time and time again

LONESOME TO THE BONE

On the park bench I slept on
Raindrops were fallin' on
The newspapers coverin' me
I hear early mornin' motors
And I know the world is wakin'
    For the dawn
But my mind's down a dark alley
Somewhere last night
    She loved me
And in the early mornin' chill
My arms remember still
But I'm droppin' like a stone
    Lonesome to the bone

The sun is roughly risin'
On the roofs of Stagger Town
The time for sweatin' poison now
Is just now comin' round
That high flyin' last night
Is over with and gone
Leavin' me
    Lonesome to the bone

I walk the way the wind blows
But any way the wind goes
Ain't good enough for me
My mind is like that traffic jam
And I walk between the cars
    Lost and alone
Your hot breath and your laughter
Keep flashing through my mind to warm me
But the naked light of day
Soon makes it fade away
And I'm goin' down alone
    Lonesome to the bone

JOHNNY CASH THE SONGS

COLD LONESOME MORNING

One of these cold lonesome mornings
    You're gonna kill me
I'm gonna lay there and I'm gonna die
You will soon give me pain enough to fill me
Cause I'm gone past doing any good to cry

And the warm sunshine is like a stranger
There's a cruel violation with the dawn
Lord, my pain can't stand illumination
And one of these cold lonesome mornings
    I'll be gone

One of these cold lonesome mornings
    Dark and early
Before a wild bird sings, I'm gonna fly
While it's dark and I'm still reaching for you
I'll wake up and I can't cry
But I know my heart can't stand another tremor
How it's holding together, I don't know
But just before the dawning's first glimmer
One of these cold lonesome mornings
    I'm gonna go

Yes, one of these cold lonesome mornings
    You're gonna kill me
I'm gonna lay there and I'm gonna die
You will soon give me pain enough to fill me
And I'm gone past doing any good to cry
And the warm sunshine is like a stranger
There's a cruel violation with the dawn
Cause my face can't stand illumination
And one of these cold lonesome mornings
    I'll be gone

IT COMES AND GOES

I been up and down and out
And I have been around
And I felt good more times than I felt bad
Lovin' you felt better than I've ever known before
Losing you's the worst pain that I've had

But it comes and goes
It's like a blue wind blows
Yes, it goes and comes
But now I'm livin' some

And today my high didn't get any lower
And my low didn't fall anymore
But sometimes when I drop my guard
   Everybody knows
Cause I can't control the feelin'
And there ain't much sign of healin'
Cause when the pain is there it always shows
   But it comes and goes

In my mind I'm holding you and loving you again
I hear you laughing, feel you cling to me
Although it's over I'm still holding on a little bit
And there's a lot of pain in the memories

TOO LITTLE, TOO LATE

So you're feelin' numb about me being gone
So now you're half alive when you're alone
Well, I just hope the pain will ease a little as you wait
  You gave me love
  But too little, too late

Dark days are comin' now, you see
Hard times for you as well as me
All-time low is comin' under your front gate
  You gave me love
  But too little, too late

So you got plans about some fine affair
Well, think about in a little while you're lyin' there
Love long and hard and don't make your lover wait
  You gave me love
  But too little, too late

SO DOGGONE LONESOME

I do my best to hide this low-down feelin'
I try to make believe there's nothing wrong
But they're always askin' me about you, darlin',
And it hurts me so to tell 'em that you're gone

If they ask me, I guess I'd be denyin'
That I've been unhappy all alone
But if they heard my heart, they'd hear it cryin'
'Where's my darlin', when's she comin' home?'

I ask myself a million times
What's right for me to do?
To try to lose my blues alone
Or hang around with you
But I think it's pretty good
Until that moon comes shinin' through,
And then I get so doggone lonesome

Time stands still when you're a-waitin'
Sometimes I think my heart is stoppin' too
One lonely hours seems forever
Sixty minutes more a-waitin' for you
But I guess I'll keep waitin till you're with me
Cause I believe that lovin' you is right
But I don't care if the sun don't rise tomorrow
If I can't have you with me tonight

I know I'll keep on loving you
Cause true love can't be killed
I ought to get you off my mind
But I guess I never will
I could have a dozen others
But I know I'd love you still
Cause I get so doggone lonesome

JOHNNY CASH THE SONGS

YOU'LL BE ALL RIGHT
(with June Carter)

Well, I see you've lost your honeybee
I know how much you must be feelin' now
    You feel sad, sad
    But, boy, it ain't that bad

You cry just a little bit
And die just a little bit
And then you'll be all right

Why, don't you know,
It wasn't that long ago,
Your honeybee
Was queen of my bee tree
And then away she flew
And took my honey to you
You cry just a little bit
And die just a little bit
And then you'll be all right

Well, I pity you
I know what you're going through
You saw your queen bee fly
Your honeycomb went dry
But if you keep pushin' on
You won't care if she's gone
You cry just a little bit
And die just a little bit
And then you'll be all right

OH, WHAT A GOOD THING WE HAD
(with June Carter)

MALE:
Sunshine and showers,
And everything comin' up daisies
Oh, what a good thing we had

BOTH:
Gone bad

MALE:
Oh, what a good thing we had

FEMALE:
Drive-ins and picnics
And every day was Saturday
Oh, what a good thing we had
   Gone bad

Long weeks of waitin'
And livin' for the day we marry
Oh, what a good thing we had
   Gone bad

The whole wide world was jealous
We wouldn't hear a thing they'd tell us
Never did need any money
Everything was milk and honey
   Oh

Long walks by the river
Talkin' 'bout livin' together
Oh, what a good thing we had
   Gone bad

CRY, CRY, CRY

Ev'rybody knows where you go when the sun goes down
I think you only live to see the lights uptown
I wasted my time when I would try, try, try
Cause when the lights have lost their glow
    You'll cry, cry, cry

Soon your sugar daddies will all be gone
You'll wake up some cold day and find you're alone
You'll call for me, but I'm gonna tell you bye, bye, bye
When I turn around and walk away
    You'll cry, cry, cry

You're gonna cry, cry, cry
    And you cry alone
When everyone's forgotten
    And you're left on your own

You're gonna cry, cry, cry

AFTER THE BALL

I hear people laughing
On the corner by the square
The moon flickers on my wall
And I know you're out there
I'm in your bed and listening
For your footsteps down the hall
And I'll be waitin' for you
    After the ball

After the ball is over
    After the ball
If you cannot stand, I've got a place
    For you to fall
The blinds are drawn and I have turned
The clock face to the wall
I'll be waitin' for you
    After the ball

Lovin' you is sweet addiction
I need only you
Just as long as you come back
Oh, do what you want to
Give the night your laughter
But I'll have you after all
I'll be waiting for you
    After the ball

LADY

Lady, your arms were always warm
And your bed was always ready
   When I came
Lady, in the middle of the night
You would open up when you heard me call your name
And you were always there to see
   The turning of my key
And your laughin' voice to me was like a song
Lady, your spirit's sweet and free
It's hangin' on with me
   Now that I'm gone

Lady, you spoke softly and kind
And you never had a word to criticize
Lady, you know I love you so
Even more than I ever let you realize
And day or night I knew
That I could bring it all to you
And if I was wrong you'd never put me down

Lady, there's so much I could say
But I can't find the way to write it down

IT'S ALL OVER

I was on my way to you when I was worried
I was all torn up and nervous
    Cause I knew that you'd gone
I knocked and crossed my fingers while I waited
And I couldn't hide my teardrops
    When I walked away alone

It's all over
It's all over
    My heart echoes
Every minute that you cry for her
Is wasted, don't you know?
It's all over
It's all over
So forget her
Stop your cryin'
Turn around
    And let her go

I was running around in circles like a baby
I was in a daze because I loved you
    So I couldn't see
I was broken in a million different pieces
When I saw enough to realize
You didn't care enough for me

I DO BELIEVE

I do believe that I won't make it through the night
If you don't come on back to me and love me now
There ain't no way that I can say that it's all right

I do believe that you're not thinkin' anyhow

But I believe if you'll remember
    How it was a little while
If you'll recall that what we had was hard to beat
And I believe that if you'll meet me
    Halfway down that second mile
We'll trade in all the bitter for the sweet

I do believe that you're not happy without me
I think you feel the way I'm feelin' without you
Come on and give in to that feelin' one more time
I do believe you won't regret it if you do

PORT OF LONELY HEARTS

A ship came in but it was empty
And then it sailed back out to sea again
Now there's a sail on the horizon
And now I wait until your ship comes in

And I'll be waiting in the port of lonely hearts
Watchin' for your topsail on the sea
Prayin' that my ship of love will come
To the port of lonely hearts where I will be

I'll brave the storm until you're with me
Cause wind and rain can't change a love that's true
I'll be alone until you anchor
And then I'll leave this lonely port with you

Till then I'm waiting in the port of lonely hearts
Watchin' for your topsail on the sea
Prayin' that my ship of love will come
To the port of lonely hearts where I will be

MEAN-EYED CAT

I give my woman half of the money at the general store
I said, 'Now, buy a little groceries and don't spend no more.'
Then she paid ten dollars for a ten-cent hat
And got some store-bought cat food for a mean-eyed cat

When I give her ten dollars for a one-way ticket
She was mad as she could be
Then I bet ten more that if she ever left
She'd come a-crawlin' back to me

When I woke up this morning and I turned my head
There wasn't a cotton-pickin' thing on her side of the bed
I found a little ole note where her head belonged
It said, 'Dear John, honey, babe, I'm long gone.'

When I heard a whistle blowin' and the big wheels a-turnin'
I was scared as I could be
I put on my overalls and I headed for town
I'm gonna bring her back to me

I asked a man down at the station if he'd seen her there
I told him all about her pretty eyes and long blonde hair
He spit his tobaccer, said, 'I'll be dad blamed,
I believe I did see her on a east-bound train.'

I bought a round-trip ticket on a east-bound train
I was broke as I could be
But when I come back I got to buy another ticket
Gonna bring her back with me

TWO-TIMIN' WOMAN

I woke up this morning
In a terrible mood
Now, you talk about a woman
Treatin' a good man rude
She had me talkin' to myself,
Gazin' at that mean ole wall
She had another daddy waitin'
Down at the end of the hall

She changes with the weather,
Like the leaves I recall
She blossoms in the spring,
But then she's gone in the fall
A two-timin' woman
With a heart of solid stone
She tells me that she loves me
But her heart's a little undergrown

Well, she drifts around the country
Like a steamboat on a foam
She said she'd never leave me
But she got the urge to roam
She never changes course
She just goes along that same old way
Well, I hope she keeps a-driftin'
Rolls along back home someday

Cause if I ever find her,
Gonna chain her to the floor
And tell her now, 'Sit there, woman,
You ain't leavin' no more.
I'm gonna tame you, mama,
Till you're eatin' from my hand,
It ain't that I don't love you, honey,
It's just to make you understand.'

THERE YOU GO

You're gonna break another heart
You're gonna tell another lie

Well, here I am and there you go
   You're gone again
I know you're gonna be the way you've always been
Breakin' hearts and tellin' lies is all you know
Another guy gives you the eye and there you go

   There you go
   You're gone again
   I should've known
   I couldn't win
   There you go
   You're by his side
   You're gonna break another heart
   You're gonna tell another lie

Because I love you so, I take much more than I should take
I want you even though I know my heart is gonna break
You fill me up and for a while I'm all aglow
Then your fickle heart sees someone else and there you go

DON'T MAKE ME GO

You take my hand and smile at me
But I can tell you'd rather be
Alone or with somebody else you know
And when your eyes look into mine
That old-time love-light doesn't shine
But let me try again, don't make me go

I want you
Don't make me go
My heart would break
I'd miss you so
Tradin' love for sympathy is old to me
What's this lovesick heart to do
When it cries for only you?
Hold me close, I love you so
Don't make me go

I'm sorry that I ever knew
The way to show my love for you
I took too much for granted all the time
Two hearts in love must give and take
When one heart fails, the other breaks
Don't make me go, I want to show this love of mine

NEXT IN LINE

The next in line will be someone who loves you
The next in line is me cause it's my time
   Now how long will it be
   Till you end my misery
You better be prepared to linger when you get to me

The time has come for you to love me, if you ever are
Come to me now so I can make you mine
   I watch them rush to you so fast
   I waited so I'd be the last
It's my time cause I'm the next in line

The next in line will want your love forever
The next in line is me and here I am
   Give me a day or two
   And I'll get through to you
You'd a-been my baby long ago if you'd turned out a few

This ole heart can't take much more waitin' for your love
I'm tired and we're runnin' short of time
   I'll make you love me more
   Then everyone before
It's my time to try cause I'm the next in line

I stood and watched you take their hearts
And break 'em one by one
   My time was comin' so
   I waited while you had your fun
Now I'm through a-waitin' way behind
It's my time cause I'm the next in line

LOVE GONE WRONG

HOW DID YOU GET AWAY FROM ME?
(with J. Carter and A. Carter)

Oh, I hate it but you made it
You're running, jumping, laughing
   Filled with glee
Oh, I told you so that I'd hold you
Just how did you get away from me?

I had bars on the window
Had you chained to the floor
And a moss-covered monster at the door
Twelve feet tall and that ain't all
And a bottomless moat with a hole in my boat
And a pit rattlesnake if you tried to make a break
Had a swarm of bees up in the trees
Just how did you get away from me?
   (You said I'd die if I tried)

Oh, where'd ya get the sense
To get through the 'lectric fence
Your handcuffs are gone, you're runnn' free
What happened to my sniper with his high-powered rifle
Just how did you get away from me?

It's true that it's you
Did you really make it through?
How about the tiger in the car?
(And dynamite you planted in the jar in the car)

Did you go like a mole through a hole?
Or did you sail like a quail on the pole?
Get into the news on TV (so I can see)
Oh, how did you get away from me?
(You said I'd die if I tried)
Oh, how did you get away from me?

THE MAN IN BLACK

MAN IN BLACK

Well, you wonder why I always dress in black,
Why you never see bright colors on my back,
And why does my appearance seem to have a somber tone
Well, there's a reason for the things that I have on

Ah, I wear the black for the poor and the beaten down
Livin' in the hopeless, hungry side of town,
I wear the black for the prisoner
   who has long paid for his crime,
But is there because he's a victim of the times

I wear the black for those who never read,
Or listened to the words that Jesus said,
About the road to happiness through love and charity,
Why, you'd think He's talking straight to you and me

Ah, we're doin' mighty fine, I do suppose,
In our streak-of-lightnin' cars and fancy clothes,
But just so we're reminded of the ones who are held back,
Up front there oughta be a man in black

I wear it for the sick and lonely old,
For the reckless ones whose bad trip left them cold,
I wear the black for mournin'
   for the lives that could have been,
Each week we lose a hundred fine young men

Ah, I wear it for the thousands who have died,
Believin' that the Lord was on their side,
And I wear it for another hundred thousand who have died
Believin' that we all were on their side

Well, there's things that never will be right, I know,
And things need changin' everywhere I go

THE MAN IN BLACK

But until we make a move to make a few things right,
You'll never see me wear a suit of white

Oh, I'd love to wear a rainbow every day,
And tell the world that everything's OK,
But I'll try to carry off a little darkness on my back,
Till things are brighter,
   I'm the man in black.

WHAT IS TRUTH?

The old man turns off the radio
Kids sure play funny music these days
   New-fangled songs!
'Everything seems so loud and wild!
It was peaceful back when I was a child!'
Well, man, could it be that the girls and the boys
Are trying to be heard above your noise?

And the lonely voice of youth cries:
   'What is truth?'

Says, 'Where did all the old songs go?
Kids sure play funny music these days.'

A little boy of three sittin' on the floor
Looks up and says: 'Daddy, what is war?'
'Son, that's when people fight and die!'
The little boy of three says: 'Daddy, why?'

A young man seventeen in school
Being taught the golden rule
By the time another year's gone around
He may have to lay his life down
Can you blame the voice of youth for asking:
   'What is truth?'

A young man sittin' on the witness stand
The man with the book says: 'Raise your hand!
Repeat after me, I solemnly swear!'
The judge looks down at his long hair
And although the young man solemnly swore
Nobody wanted to hear any more
And it really didn't matter if the truth was there,
It was the cut of his clothes and the length of his hair!
And the lonely voice of youth cries:
   'What is truth?'

THE MAN IN BLACK

PUT MY SUGAR TO BED
(with Mother Maybelle Carter)

Out pull a shrimp boat that just dropped the net
When the wind she comes a-blowin'
Worse than bad oughta get
I look southeast and, golly me, what I see
A black thundercloud with them fuzzy eyebrows
Comes lookin' direct towards Boudeleux and me

I turned to Boudeleux and me, I said,
   Put the sugar to bed
   Put the sugar to bed
Lock up the coffee and the coffeepot
Put the flour in your pillow cause it's all we got
Hang the lantern from the ceiling and watch yo' head
Oh, put the sugar to bed
Boudeleux-o, put the sugar to bed

Well, the sky she get dark and then she turned dark black
I yelled, she gonna blow one right out of the almanac
A big rain drop smacked me right on the ear
I hollar, said, hey Boudeleux but the way the wind blow
He just a soon be deaf
   He wouldn't know how to hear
I tried to call to Boudeleux but slid instead
Then me and Boudeleux put the sugar to bed

Well, the ends of that shrimpin' boat was switchin' around
She turned sideways and in-ards and out-ards and upside down
The water come in, tryin' to drown the both of us
The closet popped open and the skillet went a-flyin'
And me, I hid my head and kinda cussed
But most all crowd when she came, I said,
   Put the sugar to bed
   Put the sugar to bed

Ain't nothin' dry but my railroad watch
The salt got soggy but we still can botch
We build a fire for the coffee
    And we chickory fed
Cause me and Boudeleux put the sugar to bed
Me and Boudeleux put the sugar to bed

SHRIMPIN' SAILIN'

Well, the gulf he got a grassy bottom
Settin' where the Rockies there
And that's where I've been goin'
   For the shrimpin' sailin'
Leapin' 'cross the grassy moss
Bringing in a briney bin

Makin' poles of wond'rous waddy
For the livin' that I'm lovin'
When the creepin' crawlin'
Flippin' flappin' bobbin'
   dangle dobbin'
Sponge a file or drag a mile
Or more a course the ocean horse

Well, the gulf he got a grassy bottom
Settin' where the Rockies there
And that's where I been goin'
   For the shrimpin' sailin'
Till it's time to hollar haul 'em
Come back in with a briney bin
Of soddy bodies dressed and dandy
   Eatin' carmel candy
Makin' me and all my babies
Holdin' wads of wond'rous waddy
For the livin' that I'm lovin'
In between the shrimpin' sailin'

A WEDNESDAY CAR

The assembly line is runnin' slow on Monday
They been livin' it up and layin' up Saturday and Sunday
On Tuesday they're 'bout to come around
But they still feel bad and they're kind of down
And mad cause they still got four more days
   Before the weekend rolls around

On Wednesday they're feelin' fine again
And they're workin' like a dog and diggin' in
Tryin' to do everything they should
Puttin' them cars together good
And I got me a car that was made on Wednesday
   On Wednesday

If you're gonna to buy yourself a new car
You just better hope you're lucky enough
   To get one that's made on Wednesday

On Thursday the weekend is in sight
And they're in a hurry and they don't do nothin' right
Friday is the worst day of the week
That's the day they make the lemons, dogs and freaks
If your car was made on Friday, friend,
   You'll soon be in the creek

Cause it's payday and the loafin' has begun
Lord, them Friday cars, just hope you don't get one
Monday, Tuesday, Thursday and Friday
Are all bad days and the only tried day
   Is Wednesday
And my car was made on Wednesday
   On Wednesday

If your car wasn't made on Wednesday
I'd advise you not to even leave home in it.

THE WORLD'S GONNA FALL ON YOU

Better watch what you're doin', Henry
You better take it easy, sheriff
   Somebody might be watchin'
And the world's gonna fall on you
And the world's gonna fall on you
And the world's gonna fall on you

You can't slip around in this town, Henry
Everybody knows everybody, sheriff
Somebody's gonna tell somebody
   The world's gonna fall on you
   And the world's gonna fall on you

You better look over your shoulder, sheriff
Somebody might be watchin', Henry
You can't tell who's gonna see you
   The world's gonna fall on you
   And the world's gonna fall on you

You can't slip around in this town
Ain't no doubt, they'll find out
   You better stop that
   You better stop now
You better not wait,
   Be too late

Now, who do you think you're foolin', Henry?
Ain't nobody here sleepin', sheriff
   The whole world's watchin'
And the world's gonna fall on you
And the world's gonna fall on you

LITTLE GREEN FOUNTAIN
(with J.C. Cash)

There's a little green fountain on a little green mountain
Don't you think we oughta stop and get a drink of water?
There's a little green fountain on a little green mountain
Don't you think we oughta stop and get a drink of water?
   Oh, the water is cool and the water is blue
   A drink for me and a drink for you
   Oh, the water is cool and the water is blue
   A drink for me and a drink for you

There's a little green fountain on a little green mountain
Don't you think we oughta stop and get a drink of water?
There's a little green fountain on a little green mountain
Don't you think we oughta stop and get a drink of water?
   Oh, the water is cool and the water is deep
   Take off our shoes and cool our feet
   Oh, the water is cool and the water is deep
   Take off our shoes and cool our feet

Come along with me to the pasture
Now we'll watch the wind blow on the cows
Come along with me to the pasture
Now we'll watch the wind blow on the cows

There's a little green fountain on a little green mountain
Don't you think we oughta stop and get a drink of water?

LITTLE MAGIC GLASSES

I wish I had a pair of little magic glasses
That I could see the future
    Just by lookin' through
Then I could know which road
Tomorrow's gonna take me down
And I could see if I'll be walkin'
    Down the road with you

I would keep my little magic glasses hidden
I would let nobody else see what I see
    And everyone would want to know
    How I can know what lies ahead
And they'll wonder when I say tomorrow I see with me

But if I see into the future
And I'm on the road alone
And where the way was sunny
Now there's only rain
    I'll put them in a box
    And seal it with a lock
And I'll never take my little magic glasses
    Out again

DINOSAUR SONG
(with J.C. Cash)

Dinosaurs lived a long time ago
They were terrible lizards, don't you know
Some ate plants and some ate meat
Some ate fish and some ate beets

One was called a Diplotocus
One was bigger than your school bus
One was called a Triceratops
Three horns to stop anything that hops
Now can't you just see yourself walking along
Leading your pet Trachadon
Or feeding your Brontasaurus 'Rex'
Or scratching your Diplotocus' neck
Or riding on a Stegasaurus' back
Or swimming in a Brochiosaurux' track?
   Oh, what a time
   And oh, what fun
Playing tag with your Iguanadon

And if we had dinosaurs now
Could they get along with a horse and a cow?
Well, I wish they hadn't become extinct
Dinosaurs would be nice pets
And friends to have around
To run outside and play with every day
   Don't you think?

WATER FROM THE WELLS OF HOME
(with J.C. Cash)

As I stroll along the road to freedom
Like a gypsy in a gilded cage
My horizons have not always been bright
That's the way dreams are made

My days all run together
Like a timeless honeycomb
I find myself wishing I could drink again
    Water from the wells of home
    Water from the wells of home
    Water from the wells of home

I've seen all your shining cities
Lean against a yellow sky
I've seen the down-and-out get better
I've seen many a strong man die

Oh, the troubled hearts and the worried minds
Things that I've been shown
Keep me always returning to
    Water from the wells of home
    Water from the wells of home
    Water from the wells of home

I hope and pray that we'll drink someday
To the water from the wells of home
Lord, take me back someday
To the water from the wells of home
I want to go back someday
To the water from the wells of home

GO ON BLUES

Go on blues
Go on lonesome
Get your dark clouds
  Off of me
Go on blues
Go on trouble
Turn loose of me
Set me free

I've been down through
That valley with you
Now I've found me
Somebody who loves me too

Go on blues
Go 'way from me
Go on by me
Go on blues

Go on blues
Go on by me
Stay 'way from me
Go on blues

LEAVE THAT JUNK ALONE

Well, you come home a-feelin' for the knob on the door
You better pick up your feet, you're gonna fall on the floor
I keep on a-tellin' you, I tell you some more
    You better leave that junk alone

    And drink water
    Lawd, that liquor's hot
    Drink water
    You don't want to be a sot
    You better lay down the bottle
    And put on the top
    And drink cool H_2O

Well, your eyes are baggy and a-blood-shot red
It's been a week or two since you been in bed
You better pay attention now to what I said
    You better leave that junk alone

Well, now I forgive you for your runnin' around
If you'll just promise that you'll come unwound
I'll buy you anything you want in town
    If you'll leave that junk alone

THUNDERBALL

There's a rumble in the sky
And all the world can hear her call
They shudder at the fury
Of the mighty thunderball
The power of her engines
Now is drowned in the sea
See the deadly force from within her
Is somewhere running free

Thunderball, your fiery breath
Can burn the coldest man
And who is going to suffer
From the power in your hand
   Thunderball

Somewhere there is a man
Who could stop the thing in time
He's known by very few
But he's feared by all in crime
By courage and by fighting
He has not been known to fall
But neither has the fury
Of the mighty thunderball

Money-hungry minds need
A threat to launch a scheme
But those who hold the thunderball
Could rule the world, it seems
Cannot the peaceful world
Find the clue to where she's gone?
The silent sea won't answer now
But terror lingers on

BEFORE MY TIME

I know that hearts were lovin'
Long before I was here
And I'm not the first
To ever cry in my bed or in my beer

There were songs before there was radio
Of love that stays and love that goes
They were writing melancholy tunes
And tearful words that rhyme
Before my time
Before my time

There were songs in old dusty books
Of love that's always been
Sweet lovers in their glory
Who are now gone with the wind

Old-fashioned love words spoken then
Keep coming back around again
Nothing's changed except the names
Their love burns just like mine
Before my time
Before my time

And in the dim of yesterday
I can clearly see
That flesh and blood cried to someone
As it does to me
And there was some old song that said,
'I'll love you till I die'
Before my time
Before my time

But what the old-time masters had
Is what I feel for you
Love is love and doesn't change
In a century or two

If some way they had seen and knew
How it would be for me and you
They'd wish for love like yours
And they would wish for love like mine
Before my time
Before my time

THE MAN IN BLACK

ACKNOWLEDGEMENTS

This book would not have been possible without the great help of Bob Sullivan and Kelly Hancock, and I cannot thank them enough. Thanks also go to Jack Clement ('The Cowboy') for sharing generously his time and a song Cash had written for him, which has never been released. Thanks also to my agent, Jim Fitzgerald, to Dan O'Connor, Hugh Waddell, Madeleine Morel, the Cash family and, of course, the great Johnny Cash himself.

INDEX OF SONG TITLES

Abner Brown 210

After the Ball 338

All of God's Children Ain't Free 70

All Over Again 298

Another Song to Sing 238

Another Wide River to Cross 65

Apache Tears 135

Austin Prison 165

Baby Is Mine, The 317

Ballad of Annie Palmer, The 225

Ballad of Barbara, The 208

Beautiful Words 99

Before My Time 366

Belshazzar 62

Big Battle, The 178

Big Foot 122

Big River 250

Billy & Rex & Oral & Bob 104

Calilou 216

Call Daddy from the Mine 199

Caretaker, The 213

Certain Kind of Hurtin', A 323

Cause I Love You 312

Christmas Spirit, The 72

Christmas With You 86

Cindy, I Love You 228

Cisco Clifton's Fillin' Station 206

City Jail 166

Cold Lonesome Morning 331

Come and Ride This Train
    (medley) 146

Come In, Stranger 299

Come to the Wailing Wall 96

Committed to Parkview 256

Cotton-Pickin' Hands (with June
    Carter) 273

Country Boy 268

Country Trash 272

Croft in Clachan, A (The Ballad of
    Rob MacDunn) 176

Cry, Cry, Cry 337

Daughter of a Railroad Man 153

Dear Mrs (with Andrew J.
    Arnette Jr) 162

Destination Victoria Station 254

Dinosaur Song (with J.C. Cash) 361

Don't Make Me Go 346

Don't Step on Mother's Roses 274

Don't Take Your Guns to Town 114

Dorraine of Ponchartrain 214

Down at Drippin' Springs 258

Drink to Me 302

Drive On 192

Face of Despair 220

Field of Diamonds (with J.W. Routh) 106

Five Feet High and Rising 267

Flesh and Blood 294

Flint Arrowhead, The 113

Folsom Prison Blues 160

For the Cowboy (Jack Clement) 226

Forty Shades of Green 262

From Sea to Shining Sea 246

Frozen Four-Hundred-Pound Fair-to-Middlin' Cotton Picker, The 200

Get Rhythm 240

Gifts They Gave, The 74

Give My Love to Rose 197

Go On Blues 363

God is Not Dead 98

Going to Memphis 248

Greatest Cowboy of Them All, The 92

Half a Mile a Day 66

Hank and Joe and Me 118

Happiness is You (with June Carter) 311

Hardin Wouldn't Run 130

He Turned the Water into Wine 97

He'll Be a Friend 78

Hey, Porter 150

Hiawatha's Vision 124

Hit the Road and Go 285

How Did You Get Away from Me? (with J. Carter and A. Carter) 348

Hungry 288

Hurt So Bad 326

I Call Him (with R. Cash) 80

I Do Believe 341

I Got a Boy (and His Name Is John) 222

I Hardly Ever Sing Beer-Drinking Songs 231

I See Men Walking as Trees 82

I Still Miss Someone (with Roy Cash Jr) 324

I Walk the Line 291

I Will Rock and Roll With You 233

I'd Rather Have You 296

I'll Remember You 306

I'll Say It's True 304

I'm a Newborn Man (with J.C. Cash) 88

I'm Alright Now 301

I'm Gonna Sit on the Porch and Pick on My Old Guitar 234

I'm Gonna Try to Be That Way 77

I'm Leaving Now 322

If It Wasn't for the Wabash River 261

It Comes and Goes 332

It Was Jesus 60

It's All Over 340

Jacob Green 171

Jesus Was a Carpenter 84

Kentucky Straight 307

Lady 339

Land of Israel 61

Lately 325

Lead Me Father 59

JOHNNY CASH THE SONGS

Leave That Junk Alone 364

Legend of John Henry's Hammer,
  The (with June Carter) 141

Let the Train Whistle Blow 156

Like a Soldier 180

Little Green Fountain (with J.C.
  Cash) 359

Little Magic Glasses 360

Little Man, The 224

Locomotive Man 148

Lonesome to the Bone 330

Luther's Boogie 235

Man Comes Around, The 108

Man in Black 351

Man on the Hill, The 271

Masterpiece, The 202

Matador, The (with June
  Carter) 212

Matthew 24 (Is Knocking at the
  Door) 64

Mean As Hell 120

Mean-Eyed Cat 343

Meet Me in Heaven 107

Michigan City Howdy Do 170

Miss Tara 223

Mountain Lady 275

My Children Walk in Truth 68

My Cowboy's Last Ride 136

My Old Faded Rose (with June
  Carter) 198

My Treasure 315

Navajo 138

Nazarene 71

Ned Kelly 128

Next in Line 347

No Earthly Good 100

No, No, No 276

Oh, What a Good Thing We Had
  (with June Carter) 336

Old Apache Squaw 129

One of These Days I'm Gonna Sit
  Down and Talk to Paul 69

Over the Next Hill 90

Pickin' Time 270

Please Don't Play Red River
  Valley 232

Port of Lonely Hearts 342

Praise the Lord 81

Preacher Said, 'Jesus Said', The 94

Put My Sugar to Bed (with
  Mother Maybelle Carter) 354

Ragged Old Flag 188

Redemption 102

Reflections 126

Ridin' on the Cotton Belt 149

Rock 'n' Roll Ruby 219

Rockabilly Blues (Texas 1955) 237

Rollin' Free 284

Route #1, Box 144 175

Run Softly Blue River 310

San Quentin 168

Saturday Night in Hickman
  County 260

Send a Picture of Mother 161

Shamrock Doesn't Grow in
  California 255

Shantytown (with June Carter) 263

She's a Go-er 327

Shrimpin' Sailin' 356

Sing It Pretty, Sue 241

Singin' in Viet Nam Talkin'
Blues 190

Slow Rider 137

Smilin' Bill McCall 217

So Doggone Lonesome 334

Sold Out of Flagpoles 186

Southwind 152

Straight A's in Love 316

Strawberry Cake 252

Talking Leaves, The 132

Tell Him I'm Gone 286

Tennessee Flattop Box 239

There You Go 345

These Are My People 185

This Side of the Law 169

This Town 281

Thunderball 365

Tiger Whitehead (with N.T.
Winston) 221

Timber Man, The 204

Time and Again (with June
Carter) 329

Too Little, Too Late 333

Trail of Tears 134

Train of Love 154

Two-Timin' Woman 344

Understand Your Man 321

Walls of a Prison, The 159

Water from the Wells of Home
(with J.C. Cash) 362

We Are the Shepherds 75

Wednesday Car, A 357

Welcome Back Jesus 93

What Do I Care 300

What Is Truth? 353

What on Earth Will You Do (For
Heaven's Sake) 91

When He Comes 87

When Papa Played the Dobro 236

Whirl and the Suck, The 245

Who Kept the Sheep? (with Ezra
Carter) 76

Who's Gene Autry? 116

Wide Open Road 282

Wind Changes, The 328

Wings in the Morning 89

W-O-M-A-N 303

World's Gonna Fall on
You, The 358

You and Tennessee 205

You Beat All I Ever Saw 295

You Dreamer You (also known as
'Oh, What a Dream') 292

You Remembered Me 309

You Wild Colorado 119

You'll Be All Right (with June
Carter) 335

You'll Get Yours and I'll Get
Mine 105

You're My Baby (also known as
'Little Woolly Booger') 318

You're the Nearest Thing to
Heaven (with J. Atkins and H.
Johnson) 314

You've Got a New Light Shining in
Your Eyes 308

PERMISSIONS

The following songs are written and copyrighted by John R. Cash (unless otherwise noted) and published by House of Cash, BMI. All songs administered by Bug Music:

> 'Belshazzar', 'Big River', 'Come In, Stranger', 'Cry, Cry, Cry', 'Don't Make Me Go', 'Folsom Prison Blues', 'Get Rhythm', 'Give My Love to Rose', 'Hey, Porter', 'I Walk the Line', 'Luther's Boogie', 'My Treasure', 'Next in Line', 'Rock 'n' Roll Ruby', 'So Doggone Lonesome', 'There You Go', 'Train of Love' and 'Wide Open Road'.

The following songs are written and copyrighted by John R. Cash (unless otherwise noted) and published by Southwind Music, administered by Warner Chappell (ASCAP):

> 'A Certain Kind of Hurtin'', 'All of God's Children Ain't Free', 'All Over Again', 'Another Song to Sing', 'Apache Tears', 'Austin Prison', 'Call Daddy From the Mine', 'Cause I Love You', 'Cisco Clifton's Fillin' Station', 'Cotton-Pickin' Hands' (with June Carter), 'Don't Step on Mother's Roses', 'Don't Take Your Guns to Town', 'Dorraine of Ponchartrain,' 'Drink to Me', 'Five Feet High and Rising', 'Forty Shades of Green', 'From Sea to Shining Sea', 'Going to Memphis', 'Hank and Joe and Me', 'Happiness is You' (with June Carter), 'Hardin Wouldn't Run', 'He'll Be a Friend', 'How Did You Get Away

from Me' (with J. Carter and A. Carter), 'I Call Him' (with R. Cash), 'I Still Miss Someone' (with Roy Cash Jr), 'I'll Remember You', 'It Was Jesus', 'Lead Me Father' (originally titled 'My Prayer'), 'Leave That Junk Alone', 'Locomotive Man', 'Mean As Hell', 'My Old Faded Rose' (with June Carter), 'No, No, No', 'Oh, What a Good Thing We Had' (with June Carter), 'Old Apache Squaw', 'Pickin' Time', 'Please Don't Play Red River Valley', 'Port of Lonely Hearts', 'Put My Sugar to Bed' (with Mother Maybelle Carter), 'Run Softly Blue River', 'Send a Picture of Mother', 'Shantytown' (with June Carter), 'Shrimpin' Sailin'', 'Sing It Pretty, Sue', 'Slow Rider', 'Smilin' Bill McCall', 'Straight A's in Love', 'Tell Him I'm Gone', 'Tennessee Flattop Box', 'The Christmas Spirit', 'The Flint Arrowhead', 'The Frozen Four-Hundred-Pound Fair-to-Middlin' Cotton Picker', 'The Gifts They Gave', 'The Legend of John Henry's Hammer' (with June Carter), 'The Man on the Hill', 'The Masterpiece', 'The Talking Leaves', 'The Walls of a Prison', 'The Whirl and the Suck', 'The Wind Changes', 'Time and Again' (with June Carter), 'Two-Timin' Woman', 'Understand Your Man', 'We Are the Shepherds', 'When Papa Played the Dobro', 'Who Kept the Sheep?' (with Ezra Carter), 'You and Tennessee', 'You Beat All I Ever Saw', 'You Dreamer You' (also known as 'Oh, What a Dream'), 'You Remembered Me', 'You Wild Colorado', 'You'll Be All Right' (with June Carter), 'You're My Baby' (also known as 'Little Woolly Booger') and ''You're the Nearest Thing to Heaven' (with Jimmy Atkins and Hoyt Johnson).

The following songs are written and copyrighted by John R. Cash (unless otherwise noted) and published by Songs of Cash, ASCAP. All songs administered by Bug Music:

'A Croft in Clachan (The Ballad of Rob MacDunn)', 'A Wednesday Car', 'Abner Brown', 'After the Ball', 'Another Wide River to Cross', 'Are All the Children In' (with O. Greene), 'Beautiful Words', 'Before My Time', 'Big Foot', 'Billy & Rex & Oral & Bob', 'Calilou', 'Christmas With You', 'Cindy, I Love You', 'City Jail', 'Cold Lonesome Morning',

'Come and Ride This Train' (medley), 'Come to the Wailing Wall', 'Committed to Parkview', 'Country Boy', 'Country Trash', 'Daughter of a Railroad Man', 'Dear Mrs' (with Andrew J. Arnette Jr), 'Destination Victoria Station', 'Dinosaur Song' (with J.C. Cash), 'Down at Drippin' Springs', 'Drive On', 'Face of Despair', 'Field of Diamonds' (with J.W. Routh), 'Flesh and Blood', 'For the Cowboy', 'Go On Blues', 'God is Not Dead', 'Half a Mile a Day', 'He Turned the Water Into Wine', 'Hiawatha's Vision', 'Hit the Road and Go', 'Hungry', 'Hurt So Bad', 'I Do Believe', 'I Got a Boy (and His Name Is John)', 'I Hardly Ever Sing Beer-Drinking Songs', 'I See Men Walking as Trees', 'I Will Rock and Roll With You', 'I'd Rather Have You', 'I'll Say It's True', 'I'm a Newborn Man' (with J.C. Cash), 'I'm Alright Now', 'I'm Gonna Sit on the Porch and Pick on My Old Guitar', 'I'm Gonna Try to be That Way', 'If It Wasn't for the Wabash River', 'It Comes and Goes', 'It's All Over', 'Jacob Green', 'Jesus Was a Carpenter', 'Kentucky Straight', 'Lady', 'Land of Israel', 'Lately', 'Let the Train Whistle Blow', 'Like a Soldier', 'Little Green Fountain' (with J.C. Cash), 'Little Magic Glasses', 'Lonesome to the Bone', 'Man in Black', 'Matthew 24 (Is Knocking at the Door)', 'Mean-Eyed Cat', 'Meet Me in Heaven', 'Michigan City Howdy Do', 'Miss Tara', 'Mountain Lady', 'My Children Walk in Truth', 'My Cowboy's Last Ride', 'Navajo', 'Nazarene', 'Ned Kelly', 'No Earthly Good', 'One of These Days I'm Gonna Sit Down and Talk to Paul', 'Over the Next Hill', 'Praise the Lord', 'Ragged Old Flag', 'Redemption', 'Reflections', 'Ridin' the Cotton Belt', 'Rockabilly Blues (Texas 1955)', 'Rollin' Free', 'Route #1, Box 144', 'San Quentin', 'Saturday Night in Hickman County', 'Shamrock Doesn't Grow in California', 'She's a Go-er', 'Singin' in Viet Nam Talkin' Blues', 'Sold Out of Flagpoles', 'Southwind', 'Strawberry Cake', 'The Baby is Mine', 'The Ballad of Annie Palmer', 'The Ballad of Barbara', 'The Big Battle', 'The Caretaker' (with Gordon Jenkins), 'The Greatest Cowboy of Them All', 'The Little Man', 'The Man Comes Around', 'The Matador' (with June Carter), 'The Preacher Said, "Jesus Said"', 'The Timber Man', 'The World's Gonna Fall on You', 'These Are My People', 'This Side of the Law', 'This Town',

'Thunderball', 'Too Little, Too Late', 'Trail of Tears', 'W-O-M-A-N', 'Welcome Back Jesus', 'What Do I Care', 'What Is Truth?', 'What On Earth Will You Do (For Heaven's Sake)', 'When He Comes', 'Who's Gene Autry?', 'Wings in the Morning', 'You'll Get Yours and I'll Get Mine' and 'You've Got a New Light Shining in Your Eyes'.

'Water From the Wells of Home' was written by John R. Cash and J.C. Cash and published by Auriga Ra Music and Songs of Cash, ASCAP; 'I'm Leaving Now' was written by John R. Cash and published by Auriga Ra Music, administrated by Bug, ASCAP.

'Tiger Whitehead', written by John R. Cash and N.T. Winston, is published by Songs of Cash, ASCAP and House of Cash, BMI.

'My Friend, the Famous Person', written by Jack H. Clement, is copyright © 1991 by Clement Family Songs.

JOHNNY CASH THE SONGS